EVERYTHING CAN CHANGE IN FORTY DAYS

EVERYTHING CAN CHANGE IN FORTY DAYS

A Journey of Transformation through Christ

JEAN WATSON

For Mark—
my husband, encourager, editor-in-chief, and best friend

Printed in the United States of America

Cover design by Strange Last Name
Page design by PerfecType, Nashville, Tennessee

Watson, Jean L., 1964-
Everything can change in forty days : a journey of transformation through Christ / Jean Watson. – Frankin, Tennessee : Seedbed Publishing, ©2018.

pages ; cm.

ISBN 9781628245462 (paperback : alk. paper)
ISBN 9781628245479 (Mobi)
ISBN 9781628245486 (ePub)
ISBN 9781628245493 (uPDF) BS680.B8

1. Christian life. 2. Change--Religious aspects--Christianity. 3. Spiritual exercises. 4. Spiritual formation. 5. Devotional calendars. I. Title.

BV4501.3.W3776 2018 248.4 2018941456

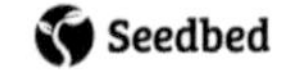

SEEDBED PUBLISHING
Franklin, Tennessee
seedbed.com

This book is lovingly dedicated to every parent
who has prayed for a child in the middle of the night,
to every husband or wife who has wept for a marriage
to be restored, to every addict who has longed to be free,
to anyone who has desperately hoped for change,

"For with God nothing will be impossible."
—Luke 1:37

Contents

Introduction

I stumbled upon the divine experiment quite unexpectedly. For more than a decade I had traveled around the world praying with people who desperately wanted to see change in their lives. I believed we were praying according to God's will as we asked the Lord for deliverance from addictions, salvation of family members, and healing in bodies, minds, and spirits. I fully expected to receive the answers we prayed for and, thankfully, we often did! However, there were other times when nothing seemed to change. I went back to the same places year after year only to find many I had prayed for no different than they were the year before.

I was also puzzled by the lack of transformation in my own life. God was using me to sing and speak of His love to many people, and I saw His power at work! He was restoring my family, and there was peace in my home. Still, I wasn't experiencing joy and peace on a regular basis. Once my daughter Katharine even joked that the words "What?" and "Oh no!"

should be emblazoned on my tombstone when I die. Funny as her words were at the time, they cut me to the core. This was not the testimony I wanted to leave my children! This was not the abundant life I read about in the Gospels.

What was I missing? I fully believed that through Jesus' sacrifice on the cross, I should have access to the riches of heaven here on earth. I preached, "Thy kingdom come," but hadn't fully experienced God's kingdom for myself. I studied the Gospels and saw Jesus spreading joy, peace, healing, and freedom everywhere He went. In the book of Acts, I read about the apostles continuing to spread the gospel message in word and in power. They saw heaven coming through their hands and knew it was Christ in them doing the work! As Paul said: "I have been crucified with Christ; it is no longer I who live, but Christ lives in me" (Gal. 2:20a).

I decided to try an experiment. What would happen if I lived like I really believed that the God who raised Jesus from the dead was dwelling inside my body? If the Spirit of the Lord was living in me all the time, my natural response would be to worship Him . . . all the time. What would happen if I stopped trying to continually fix myself and simply lived a lifestyle of worship?

I can't remember the exact date things started changing, *but things started changing!* As I began to focus on God rather than myself, the Lord began to transform my heart and my life. He taught me to see myself as He sees me and to catch His vision for my future. He set me free from the limitations of my mind that were holding me back. He gave me the courage to look at patterns of sin in my life. He taught me to pray and not give up. Most importantly, He taught me that the only thing that really matters every day is to love Him and love the one in front of me. As I stopped trying to do this faith thing on my own and let Him be God in me, my ministry grew in effectiveness. It wasn't me who spoke, sang, or played music anymore, but it was Him and I knew it. The Holy Spirit began showing up in meetings and moving hearts without me saying a word! I continued to pray for people, but I also began teaching them what I was learning about becoming the vessel that can receive God's life-transforming power. Transformation is not a magic pill we can take; it's a process of surrendering ourselves to God. Our job is to simply worship the Lord and let Him change us into the image of His Son so He can change the world through us!

The divine experiment is the kingdom of heaven coming in earthly vessels. Anything is possible for the one who is willing to say, "Your kingdom come, Your will be done . . . in me!" As we offer ourselves completely to God, He offers all of Himself to us.

> *But we all, with unveiled face, beholding as in a mirror the glory of the Lord, are being transformed into the same image from glory to glory, just as by the Spirit of the Lord. (2 Cor. 3:18)*

PART ONE

Ready for Change

DAY ONE

Forty Days and Forty Nights

Hello, new friend! Though we've never met, I can just imagine you sitting across my kitchen table relaxing with a cup of tea or French-press Columbian coffee. (OK, yes, I am a coffee snob!) Anyway, I would love to hear your story and get to know your heart. I wish I could be there to laugh with you in your joys and cry with you when your heart aches. Most of all, it would be wonderful to pray with you when you suffer because in some ways, we all suffer. Until we get to heaven life will never be perfect! We long to see change in ourselves, in those we love, and in the world around us.

Sometimes it's hard to believe that real transformation is possible. We try to fix ourselves, and we end up feeling helpless and defeated. At times our prayers seem to go unanswered. Though we might not want to admit it, sometimes it's difficult to believe that we serve a God who listens and cares.

Well, although we can't see each other right now, I hope you know that I'm in your corner. I may not know your name or understand your pain, but I know the One who does. If we invite Him to join us at the table, He will change the atmosphere of the room and even the atmosphere of our hearts! Our coffee hour can become an altar of worship as we turn to the Lord in our time of need.

As we seek God instead of focusing on our problems, He will begin to do that which He does best—transformation! However, before He can make our messy lives look a little more like heaven, He must prepare our hearts to *receive* the change He desires to bring. Will you join with me and set aside the next forty days to seek the Lord? Let's ask Him to make us into new wineskins (see Mark 2:22) so that He can fill us with His new wine!

In the Bible, God often brought change in forty days, forty weeks, or forty years. It rained forty days and nights during the great flood. Noah waited another forty days before opening a window in the ark. Moses was on the mountain for forty days seeking God, and his face shone for forty days after he came down. The Israelites spent forty years in the wilderness, one year for each day they explored the promised land. Jesus fasted for forty days in the desert, was in the tomb for forty hours after His crucifixion, and was seen on the earth forty days after His resurrection. Even a baby spends forty weeks in the womb growing from an embryo into a fully formed human being!

In each of these scenarios the Lord used forty days, weeks, or years to bring new birth, vision, and transformation. Though there is no magic in any number, if we commit ourselves to seeking God earnestly for the next forty days, He will cleanse our hearts and bring transformation exactly where we need it. He can and He will make all things new!

Let's ask the Lord to join us at the table . . .

Father, I am tired of living at a level that is so much lower than You created me to live. I've tried, but I just can't seem to change myself or those around me! Sometimes there is little I can do to change my circumstances. Lord, please prepare my heart for the change You long to bring in me and through me! In Jesus' name, amen.

1. We have asked the Lord to prepare us for change. What are some things we can do to prepare our hearts for this change?

2. Sometimes, we just need to know that we are not alone and that others have gone through what we are experiencing.

How can we be an encouragement to someone else who is struggling today?

3. Make a list of the areas where you would like to see transformation in your life. Will you commit to praying for these things every day for the next forty days?

DAY TWO

Holy Ground

Imagine that Jesus is standing in front of you at this very moment. "What would you like me to do for you?" He asks.

What would you say? If anything were possible, what would you ask Jesus to change about your life? I have asked this question many times in my travels and have yet to find anyone who does not have an answer. Even those who don't call themselves Christians somehow recognize that the name of Jesus is an invitation to believe in the impossible!

A few years ago, my brother blessed my children and me with a trip to Chicago. We enjoyed shopping (or at least window shopping) on the exclusive Magnificent Mile. We shared lovely meals and took in breathtaking views of Lake Michigan. However, all along the way we were distracted by the beggars who seemed to be constantly underfoot.

I tried to ignore them and look the other way, but soon I began to feel uneasy. So with my children pretending not to know me, I cautiously approached an older gentleman standing in front of a grocery store. He was selling magazines and holding a tin bucket that simply read, "Please help, God bless." Putting a dollar in his bucket, I looked into his eyes that were yellowed from years of alcoholism.

"What's your name?" I began.

"George," he answered.

"George, if Jesus were standing in front of you, what would you ask Him to do for you?"

There was no hesitation in his response. "I wouldn't ask Him for anything," George said. "I got saved just two weeks ago. The Lord has forgiven my sins and given me a fresh start in life. He's taught me that all I need to do is acknowledge Him every day, and He will take care of me!"

Tears welled up in my eyes and at that moment I could no longer remember the sermon I had planned to preach. The one in front of me was doing the preaching! George had chosen to seek the Lord above earthly things. Oh that my heart could be as content with nothing but God!

I then prayed a simple prayer asking God to bless him and turned to walk away. However, as I tried to leave, the Holy Spirit stopped me. "*You* go back and bless him." I knew what the Lord was saying. Reaching into my wallet, I pulled out all of my cash and handed it to him. As he looked at the roll of bills that I pressed into his hand, he wept and laughed at the same time.

"You just bought me off the street today. I can go home to my wife and pay our bills. *Thank you!*"

No amount of money could have purchased the joy I shared with George on that day. The Lord was a burning bush in our midst, and together we worshiped Him right there amid the crowd of hurried shoppers. It was a holy moment.

Instead of focusing on past failures or present circumstances, George was worshiping the One who saved him . . . *even if nothing changed.* Because his heart was seeking the Lord above his own desires, God was blessing him with peace, joy, and contentment that could never be taken away. At the same time, Jesus was also providing for his earthly needs while changing his life!

So often we seek the Lord because of what He can do for us rather than worshiping Him simply for being God. As George had discovered, placing our hope in anything or anyone but the Lord usually brings pain and emptiness. Only when we surrender to our Master's plans can our hearts be truly satisfied. Whenever we say yes to the *anything* of God, we make room in our hearts for His *everything*.

"But seek first the kingdom of God and His righteousness, and all these things shall be added to you." (Matt. 6:33)

Will you have the courage to take a moment and worship the Lord right where you are? He has an abundant life prepared for us in Christ, but most of us settle for less than His best. Today may we lay down our expectations of what we want God to do for us and ask Him for the fullness of *Christ in us, the hope of glory.*

Father, forgive me for loving my own life more than I love You. Forgive me for seeking gifts rather than seeking the Giver of all good gifts. Today I surrender my hopes, my dreams, and my desires to You and receive Your hopes, Your dreams, and Your desires for my life. In Jesus' name, amen.

1. In Jesus' first public sermon, He said, "Blessed are the poor in spirit, for theirs is the kingdom of heaven" (Matt. 5:3). What does it mean to be poor in spirit?

2. Why was Jesus able to do more miracles among the poor and destitute than among those who had wealth and stature?

3. Make a list of any dreams or desires that would be hard to give to the Lord if He asked for them. Pray for the grace to surrender everything to Him so that you may receive His very best.

DAY THREE

Receiving the Kingdom

When I noticed George on that street corner in Chicago, I had compassion on him. I had no idea what had led him to such a state of desperation, but I knew what desperation felt like. As a young violinist, I dreamed of playing in a symphony and perhaps teaching at a university, but then I made choices that were not God's best for my life. Many years later, I found my dreams unfulfilled and God's plan for my life unrealized. Instead of achieving my created purpose, I was living in a rented house as a single, divorced mother of four young children. Life was simply about survival as I struggled financially, emotionally, and spiritually.

Depression overwhelmed me and just getting through the day was a chore. As I laid in bed at night, I would imagine myself holding onto Jesus' robe and every morning I awoke with tear stains on my pillow. It was in that place of desperation that I finally hit rock bottom. Reaching for the Bible on my nightstand, I opened it and immediately saw the words, "LORD, save me!" (Ps. 116:4 NIV). Knowing I could pray that prayer, I quietly said, "God, I can't help myself because I am at zero right now. I need you to be my 100-percent God."

At that very moment, I was startled by the ringing of the phone. Picking it up, I heard a kind man ask if my name was Jean Watson and if I played the violin. This man said he had heard my name mentioned in a restaurant the night before and had begun calling all of the Watsons in the phone book until he found me. I confirmed who I was and his next words stunned me, "I want to hear you play." This chance phone call from the concertmaster of the symphony eventually led to a job as a violinist and the beginning of a new life. Although I didn't know it at the time, God was giving me a future that would not only sustain my family but also fulfill my childhood dreams!

Like George, I held out my bucket asking for help and the Lord was there ready to fill it with much more than I could have possibly asked. God longs to bring the change we so desperately need if we will only ask Him! In His first public words about Himself, Jesus quoted the prophet Isaiah:

The Spirit of the LORD is upon Me,
Because He has anointed Me
To preach the gospel to the poor;
He has sent me to heal the brokenhearted,

To proclaim liberty to the captives
And recovery of sight to the blind,
To set at liberty those who are oppressed;
To proclaim the acceptable year of the LORD
(Luke 4:18–19)

Jesus fulfilled these prophetic words as He healed the sick, raised the dead, delivered those in bondage, and saved the lost. He showed us what heaven looks like and then gave us access to all of its possibilities as we pray, "Your kingdom come. Your will be done on earth as it is in heaven" (Matt. 6:10). Transformation in our lives is not dependent on the strength of our faith. Instead, change comes when we call upon the Lord and then have the courage to answer the phone!

If you have faith as a mustard seed . . . nothing will be impossible for you. (Matt. 17:20)

Maybe you have prayed for something and nothing happened. Maybe the idea of hoping again and then being disappointed is just too scary. I can't promise that God will answer your prayers the way you desire, but I can promise that when you call upon His name, He will answer *in the way that best displays His glory.*

Let's pray for God to give us the courage to ask for the same healing, freedom, comfort, and joy that Jesus purchased for us on the cross. May the mustard seed of faith sprout in our hearts and blossom into a planting of the Lord for the display of His splendor.

Lord, give me the humility to admit that I need help. Give me the courage to call upon You with childlike faith and receive Your answers. I want to experience the full and abundant life You have for me in Christ! Be glorified in my life so others may know the transforming power of Your love. In Jesus' name, amen.

1. Jesus said in Matthew 7:7, "Ask, and it will be given to you." Why is it necessary to ask God for help? Why don't His blessings just come automatically?

2. Jesus instructed us to pray for God's kingdom to come "on earth as it is in heaven" (Matt. 6:10). Is this really possible?

3. What does heaven look like in your life today? Where do you need God's kingdom to come?

DAY FOUR

Broken Vessels

My prayer and the unexpected phone call that followed were just the beginning of the radical changes God brought into my life and the lives of my children. One day in early December, our landlord brought us a Christmas tree. As he dragged the tree into the house, he heard me singing Christmas carols on a recording I had made for a friend. He stopped frozen in his tracks, listened for a moment, and asked, "What is that?"

"Oh, that's just a gift I made for a friend," I replied.

"But, who's singing?" he persisted.

"Well . . . it's me."

He sat down on the couch, put his head in his hands, and cried. For some reason, the sound of my voice moved him deeply. Finally, he looked at me through his tears and said, "Jean Watson, I don't know what you're doing with your life, but that's what you're *supposed* to be doing!" He then gave me my rent money back and told me to use it to make a CD.

This act of kindness was the beginning of a new direction and purpose for my life. I took the money he offered, made a CD at a local recording studio, and then gave it away to anyone who would listen. I gave one to the lady at the grocery store, the cashier at the gas station, the teller at the bank, and to all my friends and relatives! Soon I was receiving invitations to sing and speak in churches and coffeehouses. I didn't really have a message in those early days except that I had made mistakes, then cried out to God, and He was changing my life.

As I traveled from town to town playing music and sharing my simple message, strange things began to happen. People had the same response to my music as my landlord. They often wept, and hearts were softened to God as they listened. The Holy Spirit moved powerfully during the concerts, and I saw people healed, saved, and set free from addictions. The kingdom of heaven was coming to earth—through a flawed, violin-playing, divorced mother of four!

So why would God use someone broken and inadequate to reveal the power of His love? Perhaps brokenness was my greatest qualification for ministry. Though I would never want to relive the years I suffered, I am thankful to have walked that road. It was necessary to be completely broken so that God could use me for His glory and not mine!

God desires to use our pain not to harm us, but rather to bring life. In His hands, pain is a tool He can use to shape us into His image. When we hurt, we can discover the treasure of His comfort even in the dark places. As we trust His love, He will use our broken dreams to bring forth His dream for us!

> *For our light affliction, which is but for a moment, is working for us a far more exceeding and eternal weight of glory. (2 Cor. 4:17)*

> *Beloved, do not think it strange concerning the fiery trial which is to try you, as though some strange thing happened to you; but rejoice to the extent that you partake of Christ's sufferings, that when His glory is revealed, you may also be glad with exceeding joy. (1 Peter 4:12–13)*

Take a moment today and give the Lord your past, your mistakes, other peoples' mistakes, your sorrows, and your fears. Ask God to take the broken pieces of your past and use them to bring His glory through every part of your life.

Thank You, Lord, that Your love is bigger than my sins and my failures. Your plan is bigger than the hurt from others, and Your faithfulness endures forever! I offer You the broken pieces of my life today and ask You to heal me and make me an instrument of healing. In Jesus' name, amen.

1. What is the difference between God causing suffering and God using suffering in our lives?

2. There are many stories about broken things being used in the Bible. Why would God use broken things to show His glory?

3. What are some practical ways you can allow God to shine His light through your cracks today?

DAY FIVE

Jars of Clay

Whether we feel ready or not, the Lord doesn't wait until we have it all together before He puts us to work. If He really does choose the foolish things of the world to shame the wise, then I must have looked pretty foolish when I started in ministry! In those days the delivery of my message was unpolished, and I sang the same songs over and over again using only background tracks, a keyboard, and a violin.

Even in those humble beginnings, though, I began to dream about what God could do through me. I remember asking myself what I would regret not doing if I had only one year left to live. I then remembered a picture I had made in ninth-grade social studies class. It was the cover of a report about Ireland simply crafted from construction paper. Decorated with pictures cut from one of my father's *National Geographic* magazines (without him knowing, of course!), this faded green memento was the physical representation of a childhood dream.

As a little girl, I was enchanted by the cultures of Great Britain and Ireland. I could even imagine myself being there when I saw pictures of those fascinating, faraway lands. As I thought about the rest of my life, I knew that something within would mourn if I lived life and never set foot on those islands across the pond. So, on a three-by-five card I wrote the words, "Ministry in England, Ireland, Scotland, and Wales," and for the next three years I carried that card with me everywhere I went! Eventually it became worn and tattered, but as impossible as this dream seemed, I continued to pray daily that God would make a way for it to become reality.

Then out of the blue one day I received an e-mail from some Christian musicians in England who had heard my music. They learned of my heart for their nation and invited me to come share His love with the British people. So after three years of praying, waiting, and believing the words on my card, I packed my bags for London with a violin on my back and a seventy-pound keyboard in tow!

One of my first concerts in England was in a small church in the city of Coventry. This city had been bombed into utter devastation during World War II and had a high rate of homelessness, drug addiction, alcoholism, and suicide. On the day of my performance, the church took a van into the city and picked up homeless men and women by offering them a meal if they would attend the concert. So that night I found myself on a tiny stage facing a reluctant audience that smelled faintly of alcohol and not so faintly of body odor!

However, the atmosphere of the room changed when I picked up the violin and began to play. A hush fell across the audience, and tears flowed freely. A man sitting in the front row stared intently at me and was first in line for prayer when the music finally ended. "I've been an atheist my whole life, but something happened tonight. I don't understand it, but somehow I know God is real!" he said. This man had come only for a meal but received so much more! He gave his heart to the Lord that night and was given a new life.

Next in the prayer line was a man and his twelve-year-old daughter. He explained that she was losing her hearing and the doctors were baffled. Speaking on her behalf, he emphatically stated, "She believes that Jesus will heal her if you pray."

I remember thinking to myself, *Well, that's probably not going to happen, but people are watching. How can I refuse to pray for her?* So I placed my hands on the girl's ears and asked the Lord to touch her through me. As I prayed, it felt like a million volts of electricity passed through us, causing me to fall backward and land on the floor!

Astonished, I stood up and exclaimed, "Get away from me! . . . I am a sinful woman. I am not worthy!" Later I remembered that Peter had uttered something similar when he realized he was in the presence of Jesus, the Christ (see

Luke 5:8). At that moment there was such intense holiness around the girl that I knew she had been healed.

Several weeks later her parents e-mailed me verification from the doctors showing that, indeed, her hearing had been restored. Absolutely no one was more surprised by her healing than me! If God could perform miracles through my hands, surely He could use anyone. That night the Lord used a broken lady to shine His healing power into broken lives in a broken city. All He asked of me was to show up and be willing.

> *For God, who said, "Let light shine out of darkness," made his light shine in our hearts to give us the light of the knowledge of God's glory displayed in the face of Christ.*
>
> *But we have this treasure in jars of clay to show that this all-surpassing power is from God and not from us. (2 Cor. 4:6–7 NIV)*

The Greek word for the phrase "jars of clay" in this passage is the word *ostrakinos*, which describes the most common everyday pottery used in that society. Often unglazed, it was full of imperfections and of little value. Yet ordinary vessels are the very ones God chooses to use. The Lord delights in bringing His glory through broken people who know they are nothing without Him. When we give ourselves to the Lord just as we are, He will use us to bring His light into the darkest of places.

Father, I offer myself to You just as I am. Bring Your light into my darkness that You might bring Your light through my darkness! Use my jar of clay to display Your glory today. In Jesus' name, amen.

1. Moses was a murderer, David was an adulterer and a murderer, and Gideon was a coward. Why does God delight in using people who have failed miserably?

2. What does poor in spirit mean to you? What is the difference between humility and low self-esteem?

3. How can we become vessels that God will use more effectively?

DAY SIX

Wait for the Vision

Over the next few years I frequently traveled back and forth to England for long weekends of ministry. Flying on Thursday night, I would pack in as many singing and speaking engagements as possible, and then fly back home to Michigan on Tuesday. I learned how to brew a proper cup of tea, drive on the left side of the road, and park in spaces the size of postage stamps! But even though I dearly loved watching the Lord's work in Great Britain, I couldn't forget my crumbling construction-paper picture of Ireland. The Lord had given me a physical picture of His vision for my life, and my spirit just couldn't rest until I saw Him bring it to pass.

Finally, one day the door opened for me to travel to the land of my dreams. Through a connection with an Irish pastor I had met in England, I gratefully accepted an invitation to visit the Emerald Isle for the first time. With tears of joy, I floated down through the clouds and stepped right into the construction-paper dream I was holding in my hands!

When I arrived, I quickly discovered that Ireland was as ready for me as I was for Ireland. Political and religious walls were coming down, and I met a whole generation of young people who had never heard the gospel. Disillusioned with the church, they were eager to hear spiritual truth. Equipped with a few Irish fiddle tunes and the Word of God, I embraced this beautiful land and its people.

Everywhere I went the Holy Spirit surprised me. It was as if I were crashing a party that had already begun. One day I walked into a church to set up my equipment and the people began to worship before I even sang or played a single note. Seeing my confusion, an Irish women laughed and said, "Jean, the funniest part is that you have no idea what is going on!" Apparently, the Lord didn't need my music or words to do His work!

One evening after a concert, I prayed with people who were hungry for God until one o'clock the next morning. As I finally packed up my equipment, a man approached me and introduced himself. He said, "I'm the program director for United Christian Broadcasting Ireland Radio, and I've watched you pour yourself out to exhaustion for the Irish people. Would you like a bigger microphone? If God has a word for Ireland, we want to hear it!"

I eagerly accepted this unexpected invitation and began speaking to Ireland through radio by recording my messages from my home in Michigan. At first these were broadcast weekly but soon they were aired several times a day. God's dreams for me were quickly coming to life!

The Lord had created me for a nation and for a calling much bigger than myself. He had trained me as a musician, gifted me as a speaker, and used my suffering to make me into a vessel He could use! Then, at just the right time, God opened the doors for me to step into the fullness of His calling.

Each of us are made to display the Lord's glory in unique ways. There are people and nations He desires to love through us and dreams only He can fulfill. As we embrace God's vision for our lives, He will give us faith to step into our destiny at just the right time.

> *"Write the vision and make it plain on tablets, that he may run who reads it. For the vision is yet for an appointed time; but at the end it will speak, and it will not lie. Though it tarries, wait for it; because it will surely come, it will not tarry."* (Hab. 2:2–3)

Ask the Lord today to remind you of *His* dreams for your life. Ask Him to make His vision clear. His leading will become like a still, small voice you cannot ignore. Then ask the Lord for the faith and courage to step into the vision in His time!

Father, I cannot become who You made me to be until I embrace Your vision for my life. Help me hear Your voice as You write Your vision upon my heart and give me faith to believe You will bring it to pass at just the right time! In Jesus' name, amen.

1. How can we know the difference between God's vision for our lives and our own?

2. Why is it impossible for us to fulfill God's plans in our own strength?

3. Take a moment to pray and then listen to the Lord. What would you be disappointed to not accomplish before you die? Write it down!

DAY SEVEN

Who God Says You Are

For years I defined myself by what *I imagined* others thought of me. Having seemingly failed to succeed in music, I truly believed I was just a mediocre musician who had nothing special to offer. As a divorced woman, I thought I was disqualified from ministry. I had long forgotten my childhood dreams of performing as a violinist and traveling to Great Britain and Ireland. Fortunately though, God had not forgotten! Little by little, He turned my life around by sending people to speak truth to me. As I began to believe who God said I was, the doors to my destiny started opening.

Everything that God does on earth begins with His Word. He spoke the world into existence. He spoke, and the Word became flesh and walked among us. And now, through Jesus' death and resurrection, God's Word can become flesh in our lives! Only as we come into agreement with who He says we are, will we become who He made us to be. Change in our lives begins as we change what we say about ourselves.

Every day we are bombarded with voices telling us who we are and what we should do, and every day we must choose which voices we listen to. Are we going to believe what others say about us, what we say about ourselves, or will we believe what God says about us?

The Lord doesn't see us as the world does, and He doesn't judge us by our outward appearance. God saw Gideon hiding from his enemies in a winepress but called him a "mighty man of valor" (Judg. 6:12). God saw a gangly shepherd boy named David who was the least of his brothers but called him "a man after His own heart" (1 Sam. 13:14). When these men believed who God said they were, they were able to accomplish mighty things!

Even Mary had a choice between believing God's voice about her identity or heeding the voices of fear and condemnation. When the angel told her she was chosen to bear God's Son she said, "Behold the maidservant of the Lord! Let it be to me according to your word" (Luke 1:38). Though others would look at her and only see a pregnant, unwed teenager, *she boldly called herself God's servant.* As she chose to believe the Lord's voice, the Word quite literally became flesh within her.

When God looks at you, He is not seeing your weakness, your shame, your mistakes, or all the things you are not. Instead, *the Lord sees the amazing possibility of Himself in you.* He already sees His power flowing in you and His glory shining through you. God will do *in you* beyond all you could ever ask or imagine if you are willing!

Today I encourage you to come into full agreement with God's plan for your life. Like Mary, His Word will become flesh in and through you as you say, "Let it be to me as You have said!" Take a moment right now to read this personalized version of Isaiah 61:1–3 out loud, placing your own name in each verse.

> *The Spirit of the Sovereign Lord in on me, because the Lord has anointed me to proclaim good news to ___________. He has sent me to bind up ___________, to proclaim freedom for ____________ and release from darkness for ___________, to proclaim the year of the Lord's favor for _____________ and the day of vengeance of our God, to comfort ___________, and provide for ___________ in Zion—to bestow on __________ a crown of beauty instead of ashes, the oil of joy instead of mourning, and a garment of praise instead of despair. _______________ will be called oaks of righteousness, a planting of the Lord for the display of His splendor.*

May you begin to see yourself as God sees you. As you fix your eyes on *who He is in you* rather than who you have been or what you have done, the Lord will bring His vision for you to life!

Father, thank You that by sending Jesus to die for my sins I now know that I am valuable to You. Help me see myself as You see me and to believe Your word for my life. Let it be to me as You have said! In Jesus' name, amen.

1. Think of the impactful words someone spoke into your life when you were just a child. Were they God's words? Were they life-giving or destructive?

2. How can we determine if someone's words about us are from God or not?

3. In Luke 1:38, Mary said of herself, "Behold the maidservant of the Lord!" Why do the things we say about ourselves matter?

PART TWO

Being the Change

DAY EIGHT

Free to Change

Over the years I have known many Christians who sincerely longed for change in their lives. Through prayer, some received the freedom we hoped for, but others just couldn't seem to get free from addiction and destructive habits. Even in my own life there have been times when I felt stuck and unable to move forward no matter how hard I tried.

If the Lord came to set us free, why is it often difficult for us to live empowered lives? Power for transformation is available to us through Christ, but it is sometimes difficult for our hearts to receive it. For us to be physically, mentally, and emotionally free, we must first be free spiritually.

The Spirit of the Sovereign Lord is on me . . . to proclaim freedom for the captives and release from darkness for the prisoners. (Isa. 61:1 NIV)

Spiritual bondage is a topic that's not often mentioned in the church. Some Christians don't even believe there is a demonic realm! The word *demon* is mentioned eighty-two times in the Bible and over a third of Jesus' ministry dealt with issues caused by demonic spirits. No, there's not a demon under every bush, but demonic forces *can* hinder us from living free and fruitful lives.

When we invite Jesus into our hearts, we are protected from evil through the blood He shed for us on the cross. This doesn't mean that evil can't affect the believer, but it does mean that nothing happens to us without God's permission. On the other hand, we can open doors to demonic influence of our own free will without realizing what we are doing. Satan gains authority in our lives through unrepentant sin, unforgiveness, involvement in the occult, believing lies, and even through the sins of our ancestors. For a more in-depth treatment of this subject, I highly recommend the book *The Steps to Freedom in Christ* by Neil T. Anderson. In this book, Anderson explains how even believers can fall into bondage and provides strategies to find freedom.

Many people I pray with have spiritual struggles that prevent them from resolving a physical or emotional problem. This certainly doesn't mean that sick people are afflicted because they have sinned. But when I see patterns of physical, emotional, and spiritual affliction that cause a person to be oppressed, I begin to ask questions about that person's past.

I have learned that spiritual bondage can be caused by something completely unintentional. For example, most people don't realize that seemingly innocent dabbling in witchcraft or the occult is extremely dangerous. Even reading your horoscope or having your fortune told is spiritually risky.

Once I met a woman who suffered from multiple ailments and was in a wheelchair. I could not understand why she didn't want prayer and even avoided me. Later I discovered she had been involved in a satanic cult earlier in her life. As a result, demonic oppression caused her to be in torment physically, emotionally, and spiritually. Unfortunately, instead of being thankful that freedom and healing was available to her, she was bitter toward God and chose to stay in bondage.

Spiritual oppression is not usually hard to spot, and if the one who is oppressed is willing, it's absolutely possible to be freed. The believer simply needs to ask the Lord for the keys to freedom. Through prayer, the Holy Spirit will reveal how the enemy gained power over us and how to kick him out! As we confess our sins and forgive those who have sinned against us, the blood of Christ covers our sin and completely sets us free. The key to freedom is having a humble heart! So many people I pray for don't experience God's abundant life because they are unwilling to receive it.

Finally, in cases where there are multiple areas of bondage or deep wounding from the past, it may be necessary to seek guidance from someone trained in prayer ministry. There is no shame in asking for help, but there is shame and loss in not seeking help. The Lord desires us to be free from addictions, destructive lifestyles, depression, and oppression. Today, let's ask God to set us free from anything that keeps us from being completely made whole!

> *Therefore if the Son makes you free, you shall be free indeed. (John 8:36)*

Lord, I want to be free to love You with all of my heart, soul, mind, and strength. Please reveal to me anything I have done to hurt You or someone else. Show me anything I have done to injure myself, knowingly or unknowingly. Please forgive me for my sins as I confess and renounce them. Set me free from all bondage to Satan and the demonic realm. In Jesus' name I pray, amen.

1. Why are many Christians afraid to talk about the influence of the demonic realm in our lives?

2. If we have fallen into spiritual bondage, does that mean we are no longer responsible for sinful behavior?

3. Ask the Lord to show you any area of your life that is not completely submitted to Him. Is there anyone from the past whom you have not forgiven? Ask for God's forgiveness and the grace to forgive others.

DAY NINE

Changed for Good

God used pain in my life to change me. Through suffering, I learned to lean on the Lord and trust Him to use all things for my good. My brokenness became my strength as I allowed the Holy Spirit to shine even through the cracks in my life! Pain doesn't automatically make us more like Jesus, however. Yes, we all suffer, but what we do with our suffering determines whether it will make us better or bitter!

Without God, pain can leave us damaged. I have met people who suffered a terrible loss, and they still carry their pain like a memorial. They nurse and feed it every day and it grows . . . every day. The pain turns into bitterness against God, against others, or even themselves. Slowly, bitterness poisons the body, the mind, and the spirit.

Bitter people are toxic to be around. When someone comes to me for prayer and I see multiple physical, emotional, and spiritual ailments, I ask questions and often find a root of bitterness deep within the person's soul. Without repentance along with a willingness to accept and forgive offenses of the past, these people are hindered from receiving the healing and life God has for them.

> *"For if you forgive other people when they sin against you, your heavenly Father will also forgive you. But if you do not forgive others their sins, your Father will not forgive your sins." (Matt. 6:14–15* NIV*)*

Bitterness and unforgiveness create a wall between us and God. Because our entire relationship with the Lord is based upon grace, we cannot receive His grace if we do not extend it to others. In fact, we will continue to live in pain when we refuse to offer forgiveness to those who have hurt us!

In Matthew 18, Jesus told a story about a servant who owed the king a great amount of money. The king forgave the man's debt, but that same man refused to forgive the debt of a fellow servant. When the king discovered this, he "delivered him to the torturers until he should pay all that was due to him. So my heavenly Father also will do to you if each of you, from his heart, does not forgive his brother his trespasses" (vv. 34–35).

I have a friend who was sexually abused as a child. When I first met her, she struggled with depression, addiction, self-harm, sexual confusion, and chronic pain. She was a Christian, but regardless of how hard she tried, she couldn't seem to find the freedom and joy she knew God had for her. Finally one day, through wise counsel and prayer at church, she realized she was ready to forgive the one who had abused her so long ago. She said that immediately it felt as if she was literally lifted off the ground! She experienced joy and freedom for the first time in years and her life was dramatically changed from that moment on. Addiction, oppression, and confusion departed and now she is happily married and experiencing daily peace.

Forgiving someone doesn't excuse evil actions. Forgiveness doesn't depend on our emotions; instead, true forgiveness chooses to release the offender from their debt to us. When Jesus hung on the cross, He had mercy on the ones who crucified Him and said, "Father, forgive them, for they do not know what they do" (Luke 23:34). In like manner, a forgiving heart has its eyes on God rather than itself.

When we forgive we are trusting God to bring good from the situation even if the one who hurt us never apologizes or seeks forgiveness. Like Joseph whose very brothers sold him into slavery, we can say by faith, "you meant evil against me; but God meant it for good, in order to bring it about as it is this day, to save many people alive" (Gen. 50:20).

God wants us to be able to experience the fullness of His love and then share it with others. As we forgive those who have offended us, we free ourselves to become vessels God can use to show His love to the world!

Father, You saw when I was treated unfairly. You were there when I was hurt and betrayed. You wept when I was abused. Give me the courage to place all my offenses and hurts into Your loving hands and trust You to use them for my good. Help me to forgive as I have been forgiven. In Jesus' name, amen.

1. Why does bitterness cause so much damage physically, emotionally, and spiritually?

2. What should we do when we don't feel like forgiving?

3. Take a moment and think about the things you have said and done in life that you regret. Thank the Lord for forgiving you and giving you a fresh start. Next, think about anyone who has offended you, and ask the Lord to help you give them the same grace you have received.

DAY TEN

Take up Your Mat

As the Lord transformed my mind and healed the wounds of my broken heart, I was eager to share what I had received with others. However, I soon learned that not everyone was ready for healing like I had experienced!

Once I met a woman at a church meeting who was blind and crippled. I thanked her for coming and asked if she would like me to pray for the Lord to heal her. To my surprise, she became angry and said, "I will be blind and crippled for the rest of my life!" And so she was until the day she died several years later.

On another occasion a lady came up to talk with me during a prayer meeting. She suffered from several different ailments causing her to endure crippling, nonstop pain. Instead of asking for prayer, she told me emphatically she did not want to be healed. She explained that her illness drew her closer to God! I told her that she didn't have to be healed but suggested we ask the Father what He wanted to do. She agreed reluctantly, so with one hand on her shoulder I prayed, "Father, what would You like to do?"

After a moment, she said, "Oh, my legs are getting rather hot!"

"Maybe He is healing you!" I responded.

I continued to pray for deliverance from spiritual bondage in the woman's heart and within moments she was completely healed from her pain. To this day her healing has remained. Healing and transformation always begin with a changed heart. Our broken hearts are like rusty buckets full of holes. The Lord can pour His love into us every day, but unless we are able to contain this love and carry it, we will never be filled. Only Christ can fix the holes in our buckets!

> *Now there is in Jerusalem by the Sheep Gate a pool, which is called in Hebrew, Bethesda, having five porches. In these lay a great multitude of sick people, blind, lame, paralyzed, waiting for the moving of the water. For an angel went down at a certain time into the pool and stirred up the water; then whoever stepped in first, after the stirring of the water, was made well of whatever disease he had. Now a certain man was there who had an infirmity thirty-eight years. When Jesus saw him lying there, and knew that he already had been in that condition a long time, He said to him, "Do you want to be made well?" (John 5:2–6)*

Notice that Jesus did not automatically heal the man by the pool; He simply asked if he wanted to be well. Desire for wholeness is the first step to receiving healing. Neediness and dependency can easily become our comfort zone. Sickness can become our identity. We must ask God to help us desire His best before we can actually receive it!

The second step in the man's healing was taking responsibility for his actions. When Jesus asked if he wanted to get well, "The sick man answered Him, 'Sir, I have no man to put me into the pool when the water is stirred up; but while I am coming, another steps down before me'" (John 5:7).

Living with a victim mentality causes us to blame others for our problems. Like the man by the pool, we can miss the grace of God if we rely only on others for our healing. We often want a quick fix to our problem, but God's plan is to heal the condition that put us there in the first place. Many times when our hearts are made right with God, healing quickly follows.

The third step in receiving healing is active obedience. Even though the crippled man at the pool of Bethesda blamed others for his condition, God still had mercy on him and offered healing if he would obey.

> *Jesus said to him, "Rise, take up your bed and walk." And immediately the man was made well, took up his bed, and walked. (John 5:8–9)*

Notice that healing occurred before the man got up, but he had to *walk in his healing to receive it.* God's healing is never just an event, it's an experience. We receive the fullness of God's love as we trust and obey what He asks us to do! We are not healed to stay where we are. Healing involves trusting God and stepping out of our comfort zone, our neediness, and our old way of life into the new way of life He has for us.

To receive healing, we must have the desire to be made well, the humility to take responsibility for our condition, and the willingness to rise up from the comfortable place where we have been lying. May the Lord heal our hearts and set us free from anything that keeps us from receiving His abundant life!

Father, I may say I want all that You have for me, but change is very scary! Please deliver me from fear or any bondage that keeps me from receiving healing and freedom in Christ. Make me whole, Lord! In Jesus' name, amen.

1. How does humility prepare our hearts to receive healing from God?

2. What is God's role in the healing process? What is our role?

3. What things are preventing you from taking up your mat?

DAY ELEVEN

Letting Go of the Past

God desires each of us to live in the freedom and joy Jesus purchased for us on the cross. However, we can't enjoy the Lord's presence today when we are dwelling in the hurts and regrets of yesterday. To move forward into the abundant life God has prepared for us, we must learn to let go of things we can no longer change.

I frequently visit prisons and have met many men and women who are locked up not just behind physical bars, but also behind the bars of their past. With way too much time on their hands, they replay in their minds over and over again past decisions they can never change.

I have also known people who grieve the loss of a loved one or a relationship and never heal regardless of how much time passes. Grief over the loss of someone they loved is slowing killing them as well! Letting go of the past must happen, however, before God's purpose for the future can be fulfilled.

In biblical times, there was a prescribed period of mourning to grieve the death of a loved one. It was appropriate to wear mourning clothes and to weep. Sometimes professional mourners were hired to weep and wail for the dead. Mourning was a healthy and necessary way to express grief and also honor the person who had passed away.

In the book of Genesis when Jacob was told his son Joseph was dead, he put on sackcloth, signifying being in a state of mourning. Deuteronomy 21 directs the Israelites to allow a girl taken captive during warfare to shave her head, cut her nails, remove her native clothing, and mourn for a month. But when the time of mourning was over, sackcloth and ashes were exchanged for fresh clothing and a new life in a new land.

Isaiah reminds us that Jesus was sent into the world, "To console those who mourn in Zion, to give them beauty for ashes, the oil of joy for mourning" (Isa. 61:3). The Lord is sympathetic to us when we mourn, but He also knows we must move forward to experience the abundant life He has called us to live!

Then He said to another, "Follow Me."

But he said, "Lord, let me first go and bury my father."

Jesus said to him, "Let the dead bury their own dead, but you go and preach the kingdom of God."

And another also said, "Lord, I will follow You, but let me first go and bid them farewell who are at my house."

But Jesus said to him, "No one, having put his hand to the plow, and looking back, is fit for the kingdom of God." (Luke 9:59–62)

Like Lot's wife, who turned into a pillar of salt after looking back as Sodom and Gomorrah burned, the Lord is telling us that looking back on what we can no longer change brings only death and fruitlessness. While our Lord is the God of the past, present, and future, we can find His presence only as we worship Him in *this moment*. If our hearts are more focused on our past failures than our present God, we rob ourselves of the life He has for us and our calling to share His life with others.

Brethren, I do not count myself to have apprehended; but one thing I do, forgetting those things which are behind and reaching forward to those things which are ahead, I press toward the goal for the prize of the upward call of God in Christ Jesus. (Phil. 3:13–14)

If you suffer with regrets or pain from the past, there is hope for you today. In Christ, you can find peace and healing in this moment and also hope and joy for the future. Jesus said, "Blessed are those who mourn, for they shall be comforted" (Matt. 5:4). Will you receive the comfort He offers? To receive God's blessings of new life, we must first let go of the old. This can be difficult, but with prayer and encouragement from others, the Lord can free us from whatever keeps us from enjoying this present moment.

Let's pray and ask God to help us let go of anything that is holding us back. As we entrust our regrets, our losses, and our loved ones to the Lord, we can trust Him to use even our past to bring life!

Father, thank You for being gracious to me in my pain. Help me heal from the wounds of the past so that in the future I may help others heal. I place my sorrows, my losses, and my regrets into Your hands and ask You to use them to bring forth life. In Jesus' name, amen.

1. The grieving process should be natural and healthy. When does grieving or yearning for the past become a hindrance to our calling in Christ?

2. Besides a death, what are some other things in our past that might rob us of God's joy in the present?

3. How can we comfort others who mourn or live with regret while encouraging them to receive the life and healing God offers today?

DAY TWELVE

Circle Your Wagons

In the beginning of my healing process, I remember feeling very weak and vulnerable. Being alone was a dangerous place for me because my emotions were all over the map! Fortunately, a very wise counselor encouraged me to circle my wagons by surrounding myself with people I could trust.

Circling the wagons was something the early American settlers did to protect themselves at night as they traveled in wagon trains. My wagons were good friends and family who were there for me when I was sad or confused. Fortunately, I had a good support system including a dear friend who called me every day to remind me how much God loved me!

In addition to the support of friends and family, my counselor recommended seeking medical help. She recognized that an antidepressant might help me manage my pain for a period of time until I was in a healthier place. Though it was hard to admit I needed help, God used the medication for a short time to bring balance to my emotions until I could once again make good decisions.

I share this so others will be encouraged to seek help and healing in whatever way the Lord chooses to provide. There is no guilt or shame in needing a doctor or medicine when we are sick. If allowed, God will often bring help in ways we never expect!

For those struggling with addiction, ongoing support and accountability are critical to avoid being pulled back into temptation. There are many wonderful resources and programs, such as Celebrate Recovery, that offer tools and support when we feel alone. Remember that God is a hands-on healer and although prayer is our most powerful resource, He also uses friends, counselors, online resources, books, and medical professionals to make us whole.

Though this book is meant to inspire hope for the miraculous in our everyday lives, I recognize that, for some, just getting out of bed in the morning can be a miracle. The first step for healing is admitting we need help. The next step is accepting God's healing in whatever form it may take.

I recently heard a sad story of a young boy who died from pneumonia simply because his parents refused to seek the medical attention he desperately needed. They were waiting on God to heal him but somehow missed the answer God provided through medicine! What a tragic and unnecessary loss. Likewise, I wonder how many times I may have forfeited the Lord's help in my life simply because I was too proud to accept it.

When Jesus walked the earth, He brought hope and healing into our broken world in a variety of ways. Sometimes He touched the sick and other times the sick touched Him. He called a dead man out of the grave and healed others who weren't even in His presence. Then after the disciples had watched Him do the miraculous, He sent them out to do the same.

> *Heal the sick, cleanse the lepers, raise the dead, cast out demons. Freely you have received, freely give. (Matt. 10:8)*

Notice how God was bringing His kingdom through ordinary people like you and me. The miracles we seek from heaven may be in the hands and words of those around us. Sometimes we just need to open our eyes and see them! May we have the grace and wisdom to recognize the Lord's help when it comes and the courage and humility to receive it.

Father, forgive me for assuming I know what I need. When life is painful, help me remember that You alone are the Great Physician. Thank You for using my brothers and sisters in Christ to be Your hands of healing and words of encouragement. Give me the faith and humility to receive Your healing in whatever way You choose to bring it. In Jesus' name, amen.

1. Why do you think Jesus healed people in so many different ways?

2. Who or what could the Lord be using to bring healing in your life? Are you accepting the healing or resisting it? Why or why not?

3. Is there someone in your life that could use words of encouragement or support in their healing process?

DAY THIRTEEN

Ears to Hear

I will always be grateful for the love and support of friends, family, and all who encouraged me on my journey of healing. Many times God used people to guide me with truth when it was hard to discern which way to go. To continue to live a changed life, I needed to learn to hear God's voice for myself. But discerning the voice of God and understanding it is easier said than done!

Jesus often said, "He who has ears to hear, let him hear," after he spoke to the crowds. He would talk about the kingdom of God using stories and word pictures while always leaving room for his listeners to ponder and interpret what He said.

And the disciples came and said to Him, "Why do You speak to them in parables?"

He answered and said to them, "Because it has been given to you to know the mysteries of the kingdom of heaven, but to them it has not been given. For whoever has, to him more will be given, and he will have abundance; but whoever does not have, even what he has will be taken away from him. Therefore I speak to them in parables, because seeing they do not see, and hearing they do not hear, nor do they understand." (Matt. 13:10–13)

In this story I have often wondered why Jesus didn't speak plainly so everyone could understand. Perhaps He knew that only those who really believed in Him would truly be listening. The ear that hears is the ear of faith; it is willing to believe even when it doesn't understand. Without faith, we cannot hear the voice of God.

By faith, we take time to seek the Lord and listen for His counsel. Taking time to seek God, read His Word, and pray for understanding shows the Lord that we love Him and that we are serious about following Him! By faith, we also listen for God's voice throughout the day. We will hear from Him when our hearts say, "Speak, for your servant is listening" (1 Sam. 3:10 NIV). The more we seek the Lord's face, the more we will hear His voice.

Sometimes we don't hear God because we are too distracted and consumed with temporal things. If we are seeking contentment without the Lord, our spiritual ears become dull over time. The more we learn to shut out the voices of the world that scream for our attention, the more we will hear from heaven.

Sometimes our ears are closed to the Lord because we simply choose not to believe. Perhaps there is an area of our lives that we're not willing to surrender to God. If we face the truth about ourselves, we may have to change! So rather than changing, we close our ears and harden our hearts.

> *"For the hearts of this people have grown dull. Their ears are hard of hearing, and their eyes they have closed, lest they should see with their eyes and hear with their ears, lest they should understand with their hearts and turn so that I should heal them." (Matt. 13:15)*

The Lord wants us to know the truth of His love and be set free in every area of our lives (see John 8:32). We are the ones who close our ears because we don't believe or are unwilling to surrender our hearts fully to Him. We are the ones who choose not to hear God's voice because deep down we don't trust His love for us! Today, may the Lord soften our hearts toward Him. May He give us ears to hear the truth of His love and hearts to receive it.

Father, forgive me for becoming hard of hearing. Forgive me for my laziness, my love of the world, and my stubbornness which keep me from hearing You. Help me yield myself to You in every way so that I can know Your will and walk in the power of Your Holy Spirit. In Jesus' name, amen.

1. Why is it impossible to hear God's voice without faith?

2. What are some things that may be hindering you from hearing God's voice?

3. What changes can you make in your lifestyle this week to create space to hear from God?

DAY FOURTEEN

Renewing Your Mind

As I walked through the darkness of depression, there were days when I felt helplessly controlled by my thoughts and emotions. Over time, however, I learned I didn't have to be the victim of my own thinking. This was especially true when my mind was filled with fear, doubt, and sadness. It was liberating to discover that just because I was thinking something didn't mean it was true! I could choose to change the focus of my thoughts and, as I did, my emotions eventually followed.

Whatever we dwell on eventually bears either positive or negative fruit in our lives. To receive the wonderful transformation God has for us, we must first bring our thoughts into alignment with His thoughts. The change we long for is already within us as we learn to *think life!*

> *For those who live according to the flesh set their minds on the things of the flesh, but those who live according to the Spirit, the things of the Spirit. For to be carnally minded is death, but to be spiritually minded is life and peace. (Rom. 8:5–6)*

The world tells us that our emotions are the result of our circumstances or the actions of others. If this is correct, the only way to be happy is to change our circumstances or change the people around us. But God's Word tells us the opposite is true—our feelings are determined by our mind-set. When we fix our minds on the Lord instead of our circumstances, our hearts quiet like a child in his mother's arms.

As our thoughts bring stability to our emotions, life no longer seems so overwhelming. We don't have to be conformed to the fears and worries of this world any longer. We can be transformed by the renewing of our minds (see Romans 12:2)!

So how do we renew our minds? Every day we are bombarded with our own thoughts and the thoughts of other people. We desperately need time to listen to God and hear His thoughts! This includes studying the Scriptures and even memorizing passages until they become part of who we are.

Renewing our minds also means setting aside time to hear from God through prayer and worship. For me, listening to worshipful music helps me direct my thoughts to higher things. Sometimes taking a walk in the woods or listening to biblical teaching online puts me in a better place. Find whatever *you* need to do to lift your thoughts to higher things.

Set your mind on things above, not on things on the earth. (Col. 3:2)

Renewing our minds means choosing to focus on that which brings life to our spirits. Satan wants us to dwell on anything that pulls us from the awareness of God's presence. If we choose to rehearse the regrets of the past, we live in the darkness instead of the light. If we fix our thoughts on our fears, we lose the peace God has for us even in the storms of life. If we focus on our hurts, we miss the grace God has for us in that moment. When we listen to that which is worthless and negative, our lives will begin to bear the fruits of death rather than life.

We are responsible for our own thoughts, and with God's help we can change our thoughts! In my own life, I have learned to change the channel when depressing or judgmental thoughts come to mind. If those around me are dwelling on the negative, I can choose to simply walk away or even change the subject.

Finally, brethren, whatever things are true, whatever things are noble, whatever things are just, whatever things are pure, whatever things are lovely, whatever things are of good report, if there is any virtue and if there is anything praiseworthy—meditate on these things. (Phil. 4:8)

There are many things only God can do for us, but there are some things we can do for ourselves. We have the freedom to decide what we think about! As we learn to meditate on higher things, the Holy Spirit will breathe life into our bodies, minds, and spirits.

Father, thank You for showing me that I can be transformed by the renewing of my mind. Today, help me look up! As I fix my gaze on You, Lord, may I reflect Your glory more and more. In Jesus' name I pray, amen.

1. How can we tell if our thoughts are of the Spirit or of the flesh?

2. What are some positive things we can do when our thoughts begin to revolve around the negative parts of life?

3. How can we discern the difference between thoughts that convict us of sin and thoughts of condemnation?

DAY FIFTEEN

Change Is in Your Tongue

My adult children love to laugh as they reminisce about the adventures of being raised by a well-meaning, but sometimes overzealous mama. Concerned about their health, I went through a phase of grinding my own wheat to make bread every day. I also made our own yogurt, canned fresh vegetables from the garden, and even attempted to make homemade soy milk—definitely not a crowd favorite!

As much as we laugh about my cooking failures, even in those early years I tried to teach my children that what came from their mouths was far more important than what they ate. If I heard name-calling, I made them speak life by saying kind words instead. Though they resented them at the time, those two words—*speak life*—were ingrained in their spirits. Words carry power . . . and they release power. Words create and words destroy. Whether we are aware of it or not, words are like a ship's rudder and have the power to influence the direction of our lives and the lives of others.

> *The tongue has the power of life and death. (Prov. 18:21a NIV)*

In the Bible, God's power was released on the earth through words. God said, "'Let there be light'; and there was light" (Gen. 1:3). Then later, Jesus came to earth as *the living Word.* He was the physical expression of the Father and His words brought light into the darkness. Just as Jesus' words brought life, Satan's words were deadly when he deceived Eve in the garden and tried to deceive Jesus on the mountaintop. In the same way, our words are seeds that either bring life or thorns that harm life. What we say impacts not only the one listening but also the one who speaks.

> *"What goes into someone's mouth does not defile them, but what comes out of their mouth, that is what defiles them." (Matt. 15:11 NIV)*

Our words release whatever is in our spirits, bringing either light or darkness into the atmosphere. Negative words hurt others while also keeping us in bondage. Complaining words prevent us from living in the blessing and joy God intends for us. Unbelieving words hinder us from fulfilling our calling in Christ. We can actually effect change in ourselves and our circumstances simply by altering what we say and how we say it!

What we say about ourselves strongly influences who we become. So who do you say you are? Who do other people say you are? Most importantly, who does God say you are? The word we speak about ourselves is the word to which we give power. Perhaps it's time to speak God's Word about yourself so that His Word becomes flesh in you!

Our words have tremendous influence on others. We can all remember comments spoken to us in the past that have impacted us forever, for good or bad. Some might have been off-the-cuff with no intention to cause pain, but they were painful nonetheless. On the other hand, good words can change the course of our lives by giving us confidence, encouragement, and direction.

Many years ago I was told I was only a "functional musician" and would never be a soloist. Believing those words, I became nervous and insecure when performing. I constantly compared myself to others and deep down inside I just didn't think I had much potential as a recording artist.

Then I found a producer who encouraged me to simply be myself. He gave me confidence and told me that my music was beautiful just the way it was. The Lord spoke truth through this producer, and my confidence grew as I became the solo artist God created me to be!

Finally, words can be used to build our faith. The greatest works the Lord ever performed in my life all came as I spoke and believed them into existence. I knew God had a purpose for me in Great Britain and Ireland, and I spoke that purpose daily for three years until, one day, I found myself walking in those lands! Does this mean we can name and claim anything we want? Of course not! Our words only bear life-giving fruit when they are God's words calling forth His will.

Do you desperately hope for change in yourself, your marriage, your children, your job, or your future? Ask God to reveal His words of truth concerning your situation and then go and speak life into your own spirit as well as your spouse and your children. Instead of bringing negativity to work, say only words of encouragement about others. Rather than complaining about your circumstances, use your mouth to praise God right where you are! Replace the regrets of your past with words of hope for your future.

Change in yourself, your relationships, and your future could be as close as your tongue! Just as I challenged my children, I encourage you to speak life this week and then watch what happens! Your words are seeds that you plant in yourself, in others, and in the world. Sow seeds of life and get ready for a great harvest!

Lord, please forgive me for being careless with my words. Help me to speak only what You would say. Help me to use my words to praise You, to build others up, and to call forth Your kingdom in this world. In Jesus' name, amen.

1. What do you think Jesus meant when He said, "But I say to you that for every idle word men speak, they will give account of it in the day of judgment. For by your words you will be justified, and by your words you will be condemned" (Matt. 12:36–37)?

2. How does this scripture affect the way you think about your words?

3. How can you use words to effect change in yourself and your relationships this week?

DAY SIXTEEN

Best Day Ever

Though I had seen God do amazing things for others in my ministry it took a while for me to find fulfillment in my personal life. I struggled with guilt and regret from the past and loneliness as a single mother. Occasionally when my children made comments about me seeming sad, I knew something was wrong! I wondered what was preventing me from living in the joy, peace, and contentment God intended me to experience. I didn't understand that these would all come *not* as my circumstances changed but rather as my perspective changed.

Early one morning a few years ago I felt the Holy Spirit speak to my heart. With my head still on the pillow and foggy from sleep, He said, "Today is the best day of your life."

What's so special about today? I wondered. *It seems like a normal day to me.*

"Live as if today is your best day ever."

Did I hear the Lord correctly, or was it just my imagination? How would I live differently if I truly believed this was the best day of my life? Well, I was traveling that day and during my flight I asked the attendant for a cup of coffee. I was nearly speechless when she handed me a cup with a napkin that read, "Best Day Ever!"

Now the Lord really had my attention! So I decided to take God up on His invitation and live as though that day really was the best day of my life. What if I cherished each moment as if it was my last? What if, instead of permitting my circumstances to determine my mood, I allowed my mood to change my circumstances? Is it possible that joy could be a choice rather than a destination?

That same day I was attending a Christian conference but was late in arriving. I slipped into the meeting room and found a seat near the back to avoid being a distraction. As the speaker ended his session and we stood to take a break, a young woman behind me tapped me on the shoulder.

She said, "Excuse me. I know we've never met, but I feel like the Lord has spoken to me about you."

"OK," I replied, a little cautious and taken aback.

"The Lord told me that your positivity changes the atmosphere in the room."

Change the atmosphere? Me? Now this day was really out of control! First, there was this random thought as I awoke, then words on a napkin, and now a message from a stranger—all happening within hours. Was peace and joy evident on my face simply because I was looking for the Lord in each moment? Perhaps joy is more than a facial expression. Perhaps true joy is the evidence of God's presence in a human heart.

In Your presence is fullness of joy. (Ps. 16:11a)

And so began an adventure in this new way of life. This was more than a power-of-positive-thinking lesson, rather the Lord was challenging me to set my mind solely on things above. I discovered that by changing my mind-set, I could find the Lord's presence in every moment and worship Him there! As I chose to thank God when things weren't going my way and praise Him regardless of how I felt, something shifted in my heart.

In the days that followed, I began to wake in the morning with a sense of expectation. What was the Lord going to do today? Where would He lead and how would He display His glory? The focus of life was no longer on me but rather on *Him*. With the psalmist I could truly say, "This is the day the LORD has made; [I] will rejoice and be glad in it" (Ps. 118:24)!

Suddenly, ordinary days seemed extraordinary. Every person I met was special, and all of my relationships seemed more precious. I became intensely thankful for things I had never noticed, and joy was plentiful as I became aware of God's presence in each moment. The decision to live the abundant life was actually creating the abundant life!

Perhaps we have been searching all this time for something we already possess. Each day that we have breath in our lungs truly *is* the best day ever if we know Jesus! With Christ dwelling in us through the gift of the Holy Spirit, we get to carry a piece of heaven on earth with us all the time. Maybe that's what Jesus meant when He taught us to pray, "Your kingdom come. Your will be done on earth as it is in heaven" (Matt. 6:10).

To experience the abundant life, we must open up the gift of *this day* and believe that the kingdom of heaven is nestled somewhere inside. Our circumstances may not be easy, but if we have the courage to unwrap each moment and say thank you, we will find the Lord's presence there with us! The key to living the best day ever is continually offering this life we've been given to our Maker in worship. As we exalt God above our challenges, our heartache, our fears, and our doubts, He will fill our hearts with His peace, His hope, and His joy!

Heavenly Father, thank You for showing me that You can change my heart as I choose to change my attitude! Help me keep my eyes fixed on You instead of my circumstances. Thank You for being my best day ever. In Jesus' name, amen.

1. How can we choose to live joyfully without denying the reality of our struggles?

2. How can adopting a best-day-ever attitude draw us closer to God?

3. How does our attitude and outlook affect our witness for Christ?

DAY SEVENTEEN

The Joy of the Lord Is Your Strength

For me, discouragement was the most challenging part of making every day the best day of my life. We all get discouraged from time to time. Perhaps things don't go the way we planned or people don't respond to us the way we had hoped. No matter how much we try to control life, things happen every day that we don't expect. So how do we deal with discouragement as Christians? Well, the apostle Paul knew all about hard times, and even though he was facing death in a Roman prison he wrote,

> *"Rejoice in the Lord always. Again I will say, rejoice!" (Phil. 4:4)*

How could Paul find anything to rejoice about in such terrible and depressing conditions? Perhaps this is the key.

Dwelling in the joy of the Lord has nothing to do with our living conditions, but it has everything to do with our perspective!

To rejoice means to choose joy regardless of our circumstances. Contrary to what the world may tell us, joy is not an emotional response. Just as John the Baptist leaped in his mother's womb when Jesus was near, *true joy is our response to the presence of God.* If we exalt God even when we don't feel like it, the Lord's presence will grow within us, and with His presence comes His joy!

I have learned that the feeling of joy comes when I make a conscious decision to trust the Lord regardless of what is happening around me. How empowering it is to know that my spiritual and emotional states are not controlled by people or situations. Whenever I feel sad or overwhelmed, I can praise the Lord anyway. In fact, those are the times when I need to praise the Lord the most! As I make an offering of praise, the Lord fills my heart with His joy.

Choosing to rejoice in the Lord doesn't mean living in denial. It's a deliberate decision to focus on Him rather than ourselves. No matter what happens, we know God has a plan and He can work all things together for our good (see Romans 8:28). Therefore, there is no reason to be discouraged. "If God is for us, who can be against us?" (Rom. 8:31).

In my ministry, some of the most joyful Christians I've met were not worshiping God in churches but rather behind prison bars. As strange as it may sound, when incarcerated men and women discover freedom in Christ, they rejoice! When they discover their sins can be forgiven, they celebrate! The joy these prisoners experience is based on God's love for them regardless of their past sins or present situation.

Oh that we could live in that kind of freedom every day! Satan wants us to believe we are held captive by our circumstances. The truth is, we have power over our circumstances when we choose to rejoice in the Lord.

> *But at midnight Paul and Silas were praying and singing hymns to God, and the prisoners were listening to them. Suddenly there was a great earthquake, so that the foundations of the prison were shaken; and immediately all the doors were opened and everyone's chains were loosed. (Acts 16:25–26)*

The chains that held Paul and Silas were broken and their prison doors opened as they joyfully praised God. Like Paul, Silas, and my friends in prison, we can overcome our circumstances by worshiping God wherever we are. When we praise God regardless of how hopeless things may look, spiritual strongholds will fall in our hearts. As we exalt the Lord above all else, especially ourselves, He sets us free from whatever our bondage may be.

Today, let's ask the Lord to help us choose to rejoice in the midst of heartache, disappointment, and every struggle we face. The joy of the Lord will be our strength as we learn to trust Him even in the fire!

Father, thank You for the example of Jesus who was joy personified even as He died on the cross. Thank You that Your joy is available to me right now no matter where I am or what I may be going through. I invite You into my suffering and pray that Your joy will be my strength! In Jesus' name, amen.

1. What is the difference between the joy of the Lord and happiness?

2. How can true joy be a force rather than a feeling?

3. How would you respond differently to pain in your life if you could actually see Jesus sitting next to you?

DAY EIGHTEEN

Give Thanks before the Miracle

I was born on the East Coast but moved to Michigan almost twenty years ago. At the time, the Midwest was about the last place I wanted to live. I didn't enjoy winters in the snow belt and I desperately missed my family in Pennsylvania. Every day in my prayers I asked God to change my location. Surely living each day as the best day ever would be easier somewhere else!

Well, the Lord did answer my prayers, but not in the way I had hoped. He clearly told me that Michigan was not a curse. It was His *gift* to me and I needed to thank Him for bringing me there. How could this uncomfortable place be a gift? Though I didn't understand at the time, I reluctantly began to thank God for Michigan instead of complaining. I even started to thank God for the parts I struggled with the most, including snow and extreme cold!

As I chose to give thanks regardless of my feelings, my heart began to change. In fact, I realized that the place I had resented was actually the place where my desires were being fulfilled! I was blessed with a job using my talents. My children and I lived in a house we loved. I had a beautiful horse to ride. Even my ministry began to blossom through unexpected divine connections! The land I had despised was becoming the land of my blessing. Could giving thanks have been a key to unlocking this blessing in my life?

In the Bible, thanksgiving often paved the way for miracles. Jesus *gave thanks* before He fed the five thousand with only five loaves and two fish (see Matthew 14:13–21). He cleansed ten lepers but only the one who returned to *give thanks* was made whole (see Luke 17:11–19).

Even on the night he was betrayed,

> *[Jesus] took a cup,* and when he had given thanks, *he gave it to them, saying, "Drink from it, all of you. This is my blood of the covenant, which is poured out for many for the forgiveness of sins." (Matt. 26:27–28* NIV, *emphasis mine)*

The disciples thought they were eating and drinking food that was perishable. However, Jesus knew that this bread and wine He lifted up represented sacrifice. As He offered up His life *with thanksgiving*, it would become life for all who would believe in Him. Thanksgiving preceded the miracle! The word *thanksgiving* literally means "to give grace," and when we give thanks to God, our hearts are prepared to receive His grace and power.

Is there an area of your life where you could use some grace? Today, instead of asking God to change your circumstances, try giving thanks *in your circumstances.* Trust God that He has a purpose for every detail of your life. The very things that are making you uncomfortable could be the very things God will use to bring transformation in you and through you!

> *Rejoice always, pray continually, give thanks in all circumstances; for this is God's will for you in Christ Jesus. (1 Thess. 5:16–18 NIV)*

Father, forgive me for complaining when things don't go my way. Help me to be thankful in my circumstances, knowing that You are working all things together for my good! I know that You will turn my trials into blessings as I give thanks to You. In Jesus' name, amen.

1. When someone thanks you for a gift you have given, how does it affect your relationship with that person?

2. How does thanksgiving change our relationship with God?

3. Make a list of the areas in your life where you are lacking. Take a moment each day to give thanks in those circumstances!

DAY NINETEEN

The Garden of Contentment

When not desiring to be anywhere other than where God had called me (Michigan), there were plenty of other distractions preventing me from enjoying life. Everywhere I turned there was something I thought I needed to be happy. All of my friends were married. Everyone seemed to have perfect children. Our family lived in a small house with one bathroom and I often had no idea how the bills would be paid. As much as God had blessed us, there was always something we didn't have! Then one day as I was driving down the road to my house, the Holy Spirit spoke to my heart. He said, "Look around. You're living in the garden."

"Lord, are you serious? This is *not* the garden of Eden. This is Michigan!"

"Look around. You're living in the garden."

As I thought about it, I began to understand. In the garden of Eden, Adam walked and talked with the Lord. Now because of Jesus' sacrifice on the cross, we are also able to live in the presence of God! He has provided a garden of contentment for us here on earth, but few find the secret of dwelling there. The gate into that garden is thankfulness and praise as we recognize that the Lord is all we need (see Psalm 100).

At the same time, there is an enemy of our souls who wants to keep us out of the garden of contentment. Just as the serpent deceived Eve, Satan will try to deceive us into thinking there is something God has neglected to give us that will make us happy. Like Adam and Eve, if we eat of the fruit of Satan's lies we will forfeit the grace God has provided through Jesus Christ.

In our Instagram world, it's easy to become jealous of what others have. There will always be someone who seems to have exactly what we want, but what we see is only a facade. When we covet, we are loving the object of our desire more than we love the Lord. In fact, jealousy and envy are really the highest form of ingratitude toward God because it's putting our will and desires above His. This is such a serious sin that when the Israelites envied Moses and Aaron in the Old Testament, the earth opened up and swallowed them (see Psalm 106:16–17)!

But if you have bitter envy and self-seeking in your hearts, do not boast and lie against the truth. This wisdom does not descend from above, but is earthly, sensual, demonic. For where envy and self-seeking exist, confusion and every evil thing are there. (James 3:14–16)

So what should we do when we see others enjoying what we wish for? To live in contentment, we must keep the Lord centered in the garden of our hearts. By choosing to worship the perfect One in the midst of our imperfect world, we are trusting Him to provide what is best for us.

Not that I speak in regard to need, for I have learned in whatever state I am, to be content. (Phil. 4:11)

Today you have the power to dismantle the plans of the enemy with the weapons of praise, thankfulness, and blessing. Discontentment can be destroyed as you praise God for being the Lord of your life. The stronghold of complaining will fall as you thank Him for His providence to you! *You call forth God's blessing in your own life as you bless those who have what you desire.* Let's ask the Lord to show us any area of our hearts that may have become hardened or ungrateful. He can change us even if our circumstances never change.

Now godliness with contentment is great gain. (1 Tim. 6:6)

Father, forgive me for looking to myself and others rather than fixing my eyes on You. Forgive me for envying what others have instead of trusting Your love completely! Help me worship You in this moment by choosing contentment and thankfulness in all You have provided. Thank You for being all I need today. In Jesus' name, amen.

1. Why does Satan try so hard to keep us from finding contentment in Christ?

2. Is it possible to find contentment without God?

3. What is the difference between comfort and contentment?

DAY TWENTY

The Lord Is Peace

Jesus must have been thinking of me when He said, "Therefore do not worry about tomorrow, for tomorrow will worry about itself" (Matt. 6:34 NIV). Learning to live in the Lord's peace rather than fear has never been easy for me. In fact, I have a history of being the "DQ" (Drama Queen) of my house! Unfortunately, my children have seen me react to unexpected situations by panicking rather than trusting God. However, at least I am not the only one who has panicked in the middle of a storm!

> *On the same day, when evening had come, He said to them [his disciples], "Let us cross over to the other side." Now when they had left the multitude, they took Him along in the boat as He was. And other little boats were also with Him. And a great windstorm arose, and the*

> *waves beat into the boat, so that it was already filling. But He was in the stern, asleep on a pillow. And they awoke Him and said to Him, "Teacher, do You not care that we are perishing?"*
> *Then He arose and rebuked the wind, and said to the sea, "Peace, be still!" And the wind ceased and there was a great calm. But He said to them, "Why are you so fearful? How is it that you have no faith?" And they feared exceedingly, and said to one another, "Who can this be, that even the wind and the sea obey Him!" (Mark 4:35–41)*

Even though the Son of God was in the boat with the disciples, they were afraid because they truly did not understand who He was. Long before Jesus was born, Isaiah prophesied that the Messiah would be called the Prince of Peace. In the book of Judges, Gideon had an encounter with the Lord and built an altar calling it "Jehovah-Shalom," which means "The Lord is peace." Peace is the very fabric of God and it is the atmosphere of His presence. The Hebrew word for *peace* is "shalom," which means "restoration, wholeness, and completeness." Christ is our Prince of Peace and through Him we can have all of these things!

We struggle to find peace simply because we really don't understand who God is and where He is. Jesus is now seated in heavenly places far above principalities and powers. He has all authority, and there is no name in heaven or on earth greater than His name (see Ephesians 1:20–21). He is in control!

Though He is seated at the right hand of the Father, our Lord promises to be with us in every storm (see Matthew 28:20). In fact, while the winds and waves are raging around us, Jesus is sleeping peacefully in our boat, completely unconcerned! As we learn to trust His love for us, fear loses its power.

> *There is no fear in love. But perfect love drives out fear, because fear has to do with punishment. The one who fears is not made perfect in love. (1 John 4:18 NIV)*

We are not fully believing the truth if we are living in fear. In fact, I have come to believe that every fear has a lie attached to it. When I am afraid there won't be enough, I am not really believing God will provide. If I fear the future, somewhere deep in my heart I'm not sure I can trust God's hand. Truly Jesus is Lord of the storm and He is with us. With the Lord in the boat, nothing can harm us!

No matter what is going on in your life today, trust that the Lord is your Jehovah-Shalom. He is your peace, your restoration, and your wholeness. Find Him in the bottom of the boat and you will rest! Cry out to Him and He will say, "Peace, be still!" to the storm in your heart.

Be anxious for nothing, but in everything by prayer and supplication, with thanksgiving, let your requests be made known to God; and the peace of God, which surpasses all understanding, will guard your hearts and minds through Christ Jesus. (Phil. 4:6–7)

You will keep him in perfect peace, whose mind is stayed on You, because he trusts in You. (Isa. 26:3)

Father, forgive me for looking at the storms instead of fixing my eyes on You. Help me take a deep breath and remember You are the great I AM in every situation I face. Help me trust and rest completely in You. Be my Jehovah-Shalom! In Jesus' name, amen.

1. How is the shalom of God more than a feeling?

2. What does it say about our relationship with God when we respond to potentially threatening situations by panicking?

3. How can we learn to look for Jesus in the storms rather than panicking?

DAY TWENTY-ONE

Resting at His Feet

Learning to cope with stress is one of my greatest challenges. As the demands in my life increase, I often push myself to work harder and end up exhausted with little to show for my efforts. I tend to focus on myself and forget that the Lord is my help and my strength. The days I press through without taking time to worship are the days I usually accomplish the least.

Jesus was always doing His Father's will but was never stressed. He healed the sick, fed the multitudes, and spent long nights in prayer. He didn't worry, and He never had to strive to make things happen. He simply lived in constant communion with His Father and did what the Lord told Him to do. Though He was working, He was also at rest in His Father's love. How I long to live in that kind of fellowship with

God! Sometimes I forget that because of the work Jesus did for me on the cross, I can.

> *There remains therefore a rest for the people of God. For he who has entered His rest has himself also ceased from his works as God did from His. (Heb. 4:9–10)*

On the seventh day, God rested from the work of creating to enjoy a relationship with His creation. Now He invites us to stop striving and enjoy our relationship with Him! We don't have to work to earn His favor. We can trust Him to take care of our needs and hear our prayers. Today, the Lord is calling us to rest at His feet and simply believe.

> *"This is the work of God, that you believe in Him whom He sent." (John 6:29)*

Once Jesus visited the home of his dear friends Mary and Martha. Mary sat at the Lord's feet listening to what He said, but Martha was distracted by the physical tasks clamoring for her attention.

> *She came to him and asked, "Lord, don't you care that my sister has left me to do the work by myself? Tell her to help me!"*

"Martha, Martha," the Lord answered, "you are worried and upset about many things, but few things are needed—or indeed only one. Mary has chosen what is better, and it will not be taken away from her." (Luke 10:40b–42 NIV)

Jesus is teaching us that worry and stress are not His will for us. Mary chose to worship the Lord in the midst of her daily life, and in His presence she received peace and rest. Martha, on the other hand, was so focused on her tasks that she failed to see the One in front of her! By striving instead of worshiping, she was missing the grace of God.

The Lord is not calling us to an inactive life, but He is calling us to a life of worship! As we focus on Him and carry His presence with us throughout the day, fear and stress will leave, anxiety and depression will leave. Who knows what healing the Lord may do in our hearts and even our bodies as we bask in His love? As we rest in the Lord, we are resting in the finished work of the cross. Everything we need is available to us through our Father's great love.

So, in a practical sense, what does it mean to rest in the Lord? It means giving the Lord first place in our hearts and not allowing worry or stress to ever take His place. To rest in the Lord means to pause in the midst of our busyness and find His presence again. We rest in the Lord when we turn our worries back into worship. He can work deeply within us as we take time to listen to His spirit and simply receive His love.

Certainly, living in the Lord's rest may be easier some days than others. But every day is a new opportunity to sit at the Master's feet and be blessed! As we worship Him in the midst of our busy lives, He will work through us mightily.

> *"I am the vine, you are the branches. He who abides in Me, and I in him, bears much fruit; for without Me you can do nothing." (John 15:5)*

Father, I want to be filled with nothing but Your Spirit. Help me stop trying so hard and just rest in You! Let my work be to worship You in all I say and do. In Jesus' name, amen.

1. Why is it sometimes hard to rest in the Lord and let Him live through us?

2. How can we know when something is done by the Holy Spirit rather than human effort?

3. Is there anything in your life that may have been done by your effort but not God's Spirit?

PART THREE

Bringing the Change

DAY TWENTY-TWO

Light in the Darkness

I've never aspired to be an evangelist. In the past, even the word *evangelism* conjured up thoughts of going door-to-door with a Bible in one hand and a gospel tract in the other. But perhaps evangelism isn't what I thought it was. God doesn't need us to convince people to believe! If we consistently let His light shine through us, He will do the rest.

Recently I was having lunch with a music producer at an Asian restaurant near Music Row in Nashville. As we ate, we talked about music and ministry and in the course of the conversation I shared stories of how God had worked in my life. After a delicious meal with good conversation, we rose from the table to leave. But as we made our way to the door, a voice behind me got my attention. "Excuse me, can you tell me how to trust God more?" said a young man in his early twenties. "I'm sorry to bother you. I just couldn't help overhearing part of your conversation. I thought maybe you could help me."

By this time, all three of us were standing in the pouring rain outside the restaurant. The man explained that he was at a crossroads in his life. Hearing my stories had inspired him to believe that perhaps God would guide him as He had me. So right there in the rain we joined hands and poured our hearts out to the Lord. We praised Him for this chance meeting and prayed for God to shine His light into the young man's darkness.

Imagine my surprise! I thought lunch was about my business, but it was really about the Lord's. Without me even knowing, God's light was shining through me on that day in the restaurant.

> *"You are the light of the world. A city that is set on a hill cannot be hidden. Nor do they light a lamp and put it under a basket, but on a lampstand, and it gives light to all who are in the house. Let your light so shine before men, that they may see your good works and glorify your Father in heaven." (Matt. 5:14–16)*

In the Old Testament, the light of the glory of God rested on the ark of the covenant in the tabernacle. In fact, everywhere the ark went, God's presence was manifested. When the Israelites carried the ark into battle, their enemies were scattered. When the Philistines placed the ark next to a statue of their god Dagon, the idol fell on its face, breaking off its head and hands (see 1 Samuel 5:1–4). When Jesus came to earth, the presence of God that had once rested on the ark of the covenant now dwelt in Him. Death had no power over the Lord, and demons and disease obeyed Him. Light and life flowed from Christ's very being, and everywhere He went people wanted to experience it for themselves.

> *In Him was life, and the life was the light of men. And the light shines in the darkness, and the darkness did not comprehend it. (John 1:4–5)*

Now because of the cross, all the power that once dwelt on the ark in the tabernacle and then in Christ Himself now rests on those who believe! With His spirit in us, God's glory is reflected in our words, our actions, and our countenance.

> *For you are the temple of the living God. As God has said: "I will dwell in them and walk among them. I will be their God, and they shall be My people." (2 Cor. 6:16)*

If we could only comprehend the power and life that is in us through Christ! As we carry His light into the world, He will draw all men to Himself (see John 12:32). All we must do is carry the Lord's presence and be sensitive to His leading.

A few years ago I was ministering in a British prison and many of the inmates received the Lord's message of salvation with great joy. As I was preparing to leave, the chaplain said, "Isn't it marvelous to just stand back, hold the Master's coat, and watch Him work?"

We don't have to convince the world to believe in Jesus. Our job is simply to display His glory and then just stand back and hold the Master's coat while He does His work! May we have boldness to speak the truth and let His light shine wherever we are! If we are willing, He will use us to bring His kingdom and change the world.

Lord, forgive me when I live for my purposes rather than Yours. I yield myself to You completely and pray that You will use me to show the world what You look like! Shine Your light through my life. In Jesus' name, amen.

1. How can we become vessels that God will use to bring His light?

2. How do we sometimes get in the Lord's way?

3. Will the Lord use us to bring His kingdom if we are not yielded to Him? Why or why not?

DAY TWENTY-THREE

Heart of Mercy

As believers in Christ, we are called to shine His light wherever we are. Though we can glorify Him in church, the Lord desires every person beyond those walls to know His love! If we are willing, God may send us into some of the darkest places where His light is needed the most. That's exactly where I found myself as I traveled to England for ministry several years ago.

The evening I arrived in Manchester, some friends had planned an outreach event in the red light district of the city. I've sung and spoken in prisons, homeless shelters, and in churches, but a street corner with prostitutes was definitely not familiar territory! Still, there was a sense of excitement in my spirit. How would the Lord show His glory on this night?

So on that cold Friday evening, four of us drove into the heart of the city and asked for the Lord to reveal His love through us. As we prayed, I saw a face in my mind. She was a young woman with blonde hair and distinct features. I thought perhaps it was just my imagination, but I shared what I had seen with the others and asked God to bring this woman to us.

Finding an empty street corner, we pulled out flasks of coffee, hot chocolate, and sandwiches, and then we waited like fishermen with baited lines. It didn't take long for women of all different nationalities and ages to step out of the night. They came like fearful children—timid but hungry for some food, a hot drink, and a caring smile. My heart ached as I saw them appear—weary faces caked with makeup, some no more than fourteen years old. Others looked hardened and tough, but it was so obvious that they all were hurting.

I stood off to the side, not quite knowing what to do, when suddenly I saw the face I had been waiting for standing across the street. I recognized her instantly. Her hair was blonde and pulled back tightly against her head. Unlike the others, she wore no makeup and the left side of her face was badly bruised. I was struck not by the bruises, but by the unmistakable beauty I saw underneath. Without thinking, I yelled out, "You are *so* beautiful!"

This lady whom I will call "Jane" caught my eye and shouted back in lower-class urban British, "No, I'm not!"

With her response, I was able to come closer and explain how the Lord had brought me all the way from America to tell her how gorgeous she was. Not sure whether I was telling the truth or crazy, Jane slowly began to open up her heart to me. She begged me not to judge her.

"I have to do this," she explained.

"I know," I reassured her. "Why don't you leave?"

"He'll kill me," she said matter-of-factly.

Wanting to trust me, Jane shared more. "He doesn't let me wear makeup. He chooses my clothes."

Partially pulling up her skirt, she showed me more bruises and an old stab wound on her leg.

"I used to believe in God," she continued, "but *that* is stronger," she said, pointing to the ground.

Still I knew something in her wanted to believe. I told her how I had seen her face as I prayed. I explained that God loved her so much that He sent me halfway across the world just to tell her how beautiful she was! Then I spoke of Jesus and how God sent His Son all the way from heaven to earth so she could have a relationship with Him.

However, I knew I couldn't convince Jane to believe in God's love. She would have to experience it for herself. I asked if I could pray with her, and she said yes. Putting my arm around her shoulders, I prayed that the Lord would reveal His love to Jane in a way she could understand. After we prayed, she looked up with tears streaming down her face and said, "Don't stop touching me. God is in your hands!"

I wondered if this was perhaps the first time Jane had ever been touched with love. This precious lady seemed to think she was too dirty to be touched, yet as I firmly embraced her I felt honored to have this privilege. This wounded woman was not worthless; she was chosen!

When it was time to go, she looked panicked. "Please don't go!" she pleaded. We gave her resources that could help get her safely out of bondage, but we had to leave Jane with the Lord that night. Though I may never know what happened to my new friend, I know she was touched by God's love and her life will never be the same! (My friends who returned to the red light district never saw Jane again. It is our prayer that she walked into the freedom Jesus had offered her!)

It is our human nature to judge those around us by their outward appearances. We see their present condition, but God sees the pain that led them to that place. We see human failure, but God sees the way to redemption.

When the religious leaders brought a woman to Jesus who was caught in adultery, they expected Him to condemn her to death for her sin. To their surprise, Jesus judged not the woman, but those who had condemned her!

> *"He who is without sin among you, let him throw a stone at her first." (John 8:7)*

The Lord never condones sin. In fact, God hates sin, but He loves the sinner. How He longs to deliver us from the pain we have caused ourselves! Jesus did not come to condemn us but rather to save us (see John 3:17)!

To be able to share the message of the gospel, we must first see as He sees and love as He loves. Just as the Lord showed me beauty in an abused prostitute, He sees beauty in each of us even beneath our scars! May the Lord cleanse our hearts from judgment so He can use us to bring His love and redemption to those who need it most.

Father, forgive me for judging others by their outward appearance. Help me see others as you see them and love them as You love them. Bring Your kingdom through me to those who need it the most! In Jesus' name, amen.

1. Why was Jesus compassionate to the woman caught in adultery but harsh to those who judged her?

2. Why is a judgmental attitude so offensive to God?

3. Is there anyone in your life who you have been tempted to judge? How can you show the Lord's love and compassion to that person?

DAY TWENTY-FOUR

Carrying His Presence

While in Ireland several years ago, I was sleeping on a train traveling from Dublin to Kilkenny. Tired from the journey, I had no intention of doing ministry at that moment. As I rested, however, I sensed someone was watching me. I cracked open one eye only to see two little Irish eyes staring intently back at me.

"Are you goin' to Kilkenny, then?" the little ginger-haired girl inquired.

"Yes," I replied, slightly annoyed.

"Do you live in Kilkenny?" she persisted.

(Realizing the Lord was up to something, I slowly woke up.)

"No, I live in America."

"America! What's it like to live in America?" she exclaimed, eyes sparkling.

Reaching into my purse, I pulled out my phone and showed her photographic evidence of my life on the other side of the ocean. We spoke about children and pets, houses and horses, and as we chatted, a loud voice interrupted us from the other end of the train car.

"Elena! Leave the woman alone!"

Obviously drunk with a beer can in her hand, the child's mother continued to yell at Elena until I politely explained that the girl was doing no harm. As Elena stayed near me with just a hint of fear showing, her mother slowly made her way closer until she, too, was looking at my pictures and listening to stories about life in Michigan. It wasn't long before the conductor announced my stop and I rose to get my violin and bags.

"Let me help you," Elena's mother offered.

Awkwardly, the three of us staggered to the coach door as the train slowed. Tears sprang to the drunk woman's eyes as she handed me my bag.

"I don't even know you . . . but I feel like you're my friend," she said.

Smiling through tears that now flowed down my cheeks as well, I looked into her eyes. "My name is Jean and I *am* your friend! May I pray with you before I go?"

Suddenly embarrassed, she lowered her eyes. "Alright," she agreed.

And so with one hand on Elena and the other on her hurting mama, I prayed. Thanking Him for allowing us to meet, I asked God to reveal His love to them. The whole encounter took less than twenty minutes, and no religious words were ever exchanged—just love shared with two hurting souls on an Irish train. I knew I would probably never see my new friends again, but joy overflowed as I realized I had just seen a little piece of the kingdom of heaven come to earth.

Jesus' presence was so full of the power and love of God that words weren't necessary. His love spontaneously touched the human condition and brought life where there was only death. Through physical contact with Jesus, people were comforted, healed, saved, and set free.

Now through the Lord's death and resurrection, we have become the body of Christ. As we learn to live in the awareness of God's presence, the atmosphere around us will be affected. When people encounter us, they will encounter Jesus!

> *For we are to God the fragrance of Christ among those who are being saved and among those who are perishing. (2 Cor. 2:15)*

Sometimes our most powerful witness for Christ comes as we just silently love those in front of us. Our job as Christians is to simply listen to the Holy Spirit and be sensitive to His promptings. How will people come to know God unless they first experience His love? May we be willing vessels through which He can touch our hurting world.

Lord, help me be aware of Your presence and sensitive to the leading of Your spirit. I yield myself completely to You and pray that You will love those around me through my hands, my words, and my prayers. May others come to know You through me! In Jesus' name, amen.

1. How can we become vessels that God will use to share His love?

2. What are some ways we might be getting in His way?

3. How can we can share the Lord's love today without preaching?

DAY TWENTY-FIVE

Hands of Comfort

Being a recording artist means spending a lot of time in Nashville, which also means spending a lot of time in the car. I think I know every rest stop, gas station, and hotel between Michigan and Tennessee! My rusty Honda Civic is showing its age, so last summer I decided to rent a car for the five-hundred-mile trek.

Normally, a rental car comes with a full tank of gas, so imagine my alarm when after only driving a couple of hours the fuel light came on and I realized the tank was nearly empty! So I prayed and asked the Lord to get me to a gas station before running out of fuel. As I rolled into the nearest station, I saw a young man standing in front of the building in great distress. He was crying and yelling into a phone for someone to call an ambulance. Concerned, I approached him and asked how I could help. He just wept and put his head in his hands. "Can I pray for you?" I asked, and he looked up with eyes that begged yes! So not knowing what to pray for, I began to plead with God for mercy, for rescue, for help, and for comfort. Somehow my heart could feel the man's anguish. As I finished, his girlfriend explained that his sister had died of a drug overdose just a few moments before I arrived.

Heartbroken, I gave the couple my contact information, and I assured them I would keep praying. I told them about my son who had overdosed twice on drugs and lived. I told them I believed God would save the young man's sister. Unfortunately, I was wrong. This time, the Lord did not answer my prayer the way I had hoped. As I drove away, I asked God the deepest question of life, "Why? Why didn't You save her?" The answer to my prayer was a deafening silence above the hum of the car engine.

In the silence, I began to understand that perhaps God had not brought me there for the girl but rather for her brother. What are the chances my rental car would run out of gas in that place at the exact moment she would die? God so loved this young man that He sent the Holy Spirit, the Comforter, to bring comfort through me! He experienced the compassion of Jesus that day—Emmanuel, God with us. Until we reach heaven, we will live with pain, disease, death, and disappointment. Jesus did not come to take away our sorrow, *He came to enter into our sorrow and bear it with us.*

> *Surely He has borne our griefs and carried our sorrows. (Isa. 53:4a)*

When we pray, sometimes we receive the answer we desire and sometimes we don't. The kingdom of heaven isn't always about the happy answer! The kingdom of heaven is the presence of God with us in every moment—in our joys and especially in our sorrows. As Christians, we are not called or even able to fix the world's problems. We are called to share in the world's sorrows and bring God's comfort.

> *Blessed be the God and Father of our Lord Jesus Christ, the Father of mercies and God of all comfort, who comforts us in all our tribulation, that we may be able to comfort those who are in any trouble, with the comfort with which we ourselves are comforted by God. (2 Cor. 1:3–4)*

Perhaps the glory of God is not always revealed in a flashy display of power. Maybe the glory of God is a hand on a weary shoulder or a prayer on the side of a lonely road. How merciful of the Lord to reveal His great love to us when we need it most and then use us to share His love with our hurting world.

Father, thank You for sending Your only Son to die that we might have life through You. Thank You for giving Your Spirit to comfort us and that You comfort others through us. Use us today to show Your love to someone who needs it! In Christ's name, amen.

1. How can bringing comfort to someone who is hurting reveal God's love?

2. How can loving the one in front of us change us as well as the one who is loved?

3. What are some ways the Lord revealed His love to you when you needed it the most?

DAY TWENTY-SIX

Acts of Kindness

One summer a few years ago there was a man selling peaches and watermelons on the side of the road near my house. I noticed him and wondered about his life as he stood in the hot sun day after day.

Finally, as I was driving past this man yet again, I felt the Lord leading me to stop and give him some money. Knowing I had heard from God, I pulled off the road and told the man I wanted to buy some peaches. As he eagerly bagged them up, I also explained that the Lord had told me to bless him with some extra money.

I wish I had taken a picture of his response. His face erupted with a look of shock, disbelief, and joy all at the same time! He wept and then said he knew God had sent me—not to give him money but to pray for him. He explained that he was going to trial the next day for a crime he didn't commit.

He believed with all of his heart that I had been sent by God to pray for him. The man dusted off his chair and motioned for me to sit, and together we asked God to be his strength and defender. What joy I received knowing I participated in a miracle just by stopping to buy peaches!

It wasn't difficult for me to show kindness to this man I had never met. He had never done anything to hurt or offend me. But real kindness shows mercy even to the one who deserves punishment and pays the debts of the one who can never repay. It delights in giving without expecting anything in return. Kindness was Jesus hanging on a cross praying for those who crucified Him by saying, "Father, forgive them, for they do not know what they do" (Luke 23:34).

Jesus wasn't afraid to roll up His sleeves and get dirty. He touched lepers, He spat on mud and then smeared it on a blind man's eyes, and He washed His disciples' filthy feet. That one always gets me. Feet can take a beating and I don't want anyone washing mine! But this was how Jesus demonstrated what love really looks like. He was even born in a manure-filled barn just to show us there is no struggle He isn't willing to share with us. True love expresses itself by coming alongside someone in their weakness, even at its own expense, and then sharing their burden. That is what the Lord does—He is kind to us in our frailty and covers our faults instead of condemning us.

In the ages to come He might show the exceeding riches of His grace in His kindness toward us in Christ Jesus. (Eph. 2:7)

The more I discover the kindness of our Savior, the more I want to share His kindness with others. The world may tell us that kindness sounds passive and weak, but it's actually a powerful weapon fueled by love that totally disarms the powers of darkness! When we practice kindness by laying down our lives for others, we enable God's love to touch someone personally. That is power. That is influence. That is victory!

Kindness can be shown as a gift given, a helpful deed, or an encouraging word with no judgment or strings attached. Personally, when I have stepped out of my selfishness and been kind, even when offended or hurt (especially when offended or hurt), I have seen God change the hardest of hearts!

Therefore, as the elect of God, holy and beloved, put on tender mercies, kindness, humility, meekness, longsuffering; bearing with one another, and forgiving one another, if anyone has a complaint against another; even as Christ forgave you, so you also must do. But above all these things put on love, which is the bond of perfection. (Col. 3:12–14)

Kindness is the evidence of God's love, which breaks down barriers of the heart. Today let it shine through your eyes, touch through your hands, and bless with your words. Give, holding nothing back and expecting nothing in return. Who knows what the Lord may do through you as you let His love flow?

Father, forgive me for my selfishness. Thank You for showing me what kindness looks like through the gift of Your Son Jesus Christ. Help me to truly be kind today to everyone I meet. Help me be especially kind to those who are hurting and those who have hurt me. Express Your love to others through me. I pray in Jesus' name, amen.

1. When is kindness easy? When is it most difficult?

2. How can kindness demonstrate the love of Jesus to others?

3. Why does kindness disarm Satan?

DAY TWENTY-SEVEN

The Least of These

It's challenging to be a musician in ministry. Even those who are called to this lifestyle know the dilemma of balancing ministry and personal dreams.

In a town like Nashville, where music and fame are prized above all, it's easy to be lured into a desire for recognition. As Christians, we begin this journey with the motive of bringing glory to God through our music. If we're not careful though, we can lose track of our calling and in subtle ways begin to seek glory for ourselves.

When I first started singing and then later recording, I assumed I knew what ministry was. I was on the road telling people about the love of God while also sharing my heart through music. Without realizing it, I began to think of myself as special and anointed and possibly even spiritually superior, though I would never have admitted it! I was rejoicing in all God was doing through me, but deep down inside I also wanted the credit!

I remember singing for a church in England one morning. As I left the service feeling quite pleased with myself, a man came up to me saying that he had a word from the Lord for me. Thinking how pleased God must be with *my* ministry, I said, "OK, what is it?" Soberly he said, "In the Bible, God used a donkey and God used a great fish. He doesn't need you."

His words stunned me, but I thanked the man anyway and walked away shaken to my core. Though his message was not easy to hear, I knew it was true. I was doing God's work, but the Lord was not concerned with what I did. He cared about why I did it.

The world tells us that to be successful we must be seen, recognized, and praised. God's way is the opposite; to go higher, we must go lower. God's genuine authority is always carried with meekness and obedience.

Remember David who defeated Goliath with a single stone? The young shepherd boy had no idea he was going to face a giant when God called him to the battlefield. He was simply told to go and carry food to his brothers!

> *Then Jesse said to his son David, "Take now for your brothers an ephah of this dried grain and these*

ten loaves, and run to your brothers at the camp." (1 Sam. 17:17)

Just imagine what David must have been thinking. He had been anointed above all of his brothers by the high priest Samuel. When his father told him to deliver food to his brothers, he could have refused to do such a menial task. David would receive no recognition for this task. In fact, his obedience went completely unnoticed by man—but God noticed!

In David's humility, the Lord saw the heart of a king because he saw the heart of one willing to serve! On that day the real victory had nothing to do with slaying a giant. David proved himself worthy to carry God's anointing as he willingly carried a basket of roasted grain to his unappreciative brothers. In less than twenty-four hours, he went from being a freckled-faced shepherd boy to a mighty warrior known across Israel and across the centuries! As Jesus would later demonstrate for us, the key to promotion in God's kingdom is humility, service, and obedience.

Jesus, knowing that the Father had given all things into His hands, and that He had come from God and was going to God, rose from supper and laid aside His garments, took a towel and girded Himself. After that,

He poured water into a basin and began to wash the disciples' feet, and to wipe them with the towel with which He was girded. (John 13:3–5)

Many desire the glory and praise of the warrior who slays the giant, but few are willing to serve. How many of us would lay down our lives for those who seek to hurt us or hurt those we love? Yet Jesus tells us that "whoever desires to save his life will lose it, but whoever loses his life for My sake will find it" (Matt. 16:25).

For God to use us to do great things, we must first learn to obey Him in the small things. Change will come in our homes, work, and ministry as we assume the lowest place. Will you have courage with me this week? Will you do whatever God asks of you even if it involves making yourself nothing? If, like Jesus, we have the meekness to get on our knees and wash feet, the Lord will use us for His glory.

Father, I know You created me with a holy calling. Forgive me for trying to fulfill Your calling in my own strength. Help me to faithfully serve wherever You send me. Make me a vessel that can be used to bring You glory! In Christ's name I pray, amen.

1. Jesus said in Matthew 7:21–23, "Not everyone who says to Me, 'Lord, Lord,' shall enter the kingdom of heaven, but

he who does the will of My Father in heaven. Many will say to Me in that day, 'Lord, Lord, have we not prophesied in Your name, cast out demons in Your name, and done many wonders in Your name?' And then I will declare to them, 'I never knew you; depart from Me, you who practice lawlessness.'" This is a hard scripture! Is it possible to do the Lord's work but not be in His will?

2. Why is pride such a serious sin in God's eyes?

3. How can we know we are serving God with pure motives?

DAY TWENTY-EIGHT

Faithful in Small Things

Above my kitchen sink hangs a little plaque which reads:

> *"Well done, good and faithful servant; you were faithful over a few things, I will make you ruler over many things. Enter the joy of your [L]ord." (Matt. 25:21)*

I need to see those words as I wash dishes—one of my least favorite chores! Could the key to entering into the fullness of our calling lie in being faithful with what is in our hands at the moment . . . even if it's dirty dishes?

As servants, our role is to serve the will of someone else before serving ourselves. Being a *faithful servant* implies working with our whole heart to bring pleasure to the one we serve. Faithfulness tells not what has been done, but why it was done. Through this parable, Jesus is telling us that the key to overcoming our circumstances is being faithful in our circumstances!

One of the greatest examples of faithfulness I know is the story of Joseph in the book of Genesis. As a young man of great dreams and position, Joseph lost everything when he was sold into slavery by his own brothers. Still, rather than being overcome by sorrow and bitterness, Joseph gave his very best to please his earthly masters! Because of his faithfulness, God's favor rested on him wherever he served.

> *The LORD was with Joseph, and he was a successful man; and he was in the house of his master the Egyptian. And his master saw that the LORD was with him and that the LORD made all he did to prosper in his hand. So Joseph found favor in his sight, and served him. Then he made him overseer of his house, and all that he had he put under his authority. (Gen. 39:2–4)*

Joseph was faithful in the small things and was given more! His character continued to be tested when he was falsely accused by Potiphar's wife and thrown into prison for a crime he didn't commit. Through it all he remained faithful and continued to find favor with both God and man.

> *But the Lord was with Joseph and showed him mercy, and He gave him favor in the sight of the keeper of the prison. And the keeper of the prison committed to Joseph's hand all the prisoners who were in the prison; whatever they did there, it was his doing. The keeper of the prison did not look into anything that was under Joseph's authority, because the Lord was with him; and whatever he did, the Lord made it prosper.* (Gen. 39:21–23)

Although he didn't know it at the time, the Lord was developing character in Joseph to prepare him to carry authority. There would come a day when he would be second in power only to Pharaoh himself! In the end, Joseph knew it was God's favor that had opened this door of opportunity. Looking back, he could see how God had used his suffering for good! When his brothers finally came to him asking for forgiveness, he said,

> *But as for you, you meant evil against me; but God meant it for good, in order to bring it about as it is this day, to save many people alive.* (Gen. 50:20)

Faithfulness doesn't complain about circumstances; instead, it trusts that the Master will use those circumstances for good. Faithfulness doesn't seek to please itself, but rather it uses whatever is in its hands to please God.

I wonder what would happen if we stopped complaining about the dirty dishes in our lives. What if we washed and polished them for the glory of God? Of course I'm not talking about dishwashing liquid, but rather about the attitude of our hearts. As we are faithful to serve wherever God has placed us, His favor will rest upon us for promotion! As we seek to please Him, the Lord will bless whatever we put our hands to for His glory. *As we entrust ourselves to the Lord, He entrusts even more to us.*

I hope you are excited. The things that have held you back could be the very things God will use to propel you forward! Whatever our hands find to do, may we do all for the glory of God.

Father, so often my love for You is not enough. I so easily forget that You have a purpose for allowing me to be where I am in life at this moment. Help me be faithful in the place I am planted and trust that You are working through me. Use all that I have and all that I am for Your glory. In Jesus' name, amen.

1. What does Joseph's story teach us about the source of joy?

2. How should we respond when earthly masters treat us unfairly?

3. What are some practical ways you can be an overcomer in your present circumstances?

DAY TWENTY-NINE

Choosing God's Best

After my divorce, I had a series of relationships that were not God's best for me or my children. Realizing I had let my emotions lead me astray in the past, I asked the Lord to protect me from any path that was not His perfect will. Well, God's best path turned out to be much longer and more difficult than I ever thought I could bear!

Then one day I met a man who seemed perfect. He seemed to love God and love me. He could provide for me and cared for my children. I loved him and believed surely he was the one! But as much as I desired marriage, our relationship seemed to face one roadblock after another. His children initially did not accept me and my children were wary. My friends and family noticed red flags, but I refused to listen to any voices that were contrary to what I desired.

After two years my heart was unchanged, yet we were still not progressing toward the marriage of which I had dreamed. Every time we moved past one roadblock, a new one appeared. One day I felt the Lord urging me to make a list of the fruit this relationship was bearing in my life. So I closed my eyes, took a deep breath, and faced the truth. Instead of the peace, love, and joy one would expect when two people are preparing for marriage, all I saw was confusion, strife, pain, depression, and anger. Though I didn't want to admit it, deep inside I knew these were not the fruits of the Holy Spirit.

Without confidence to move forward, but yet not strong enough to end the relationship, I clearly heard the Lord ask me to step away from it for a full year. It felt as though I was cutting off my right arm, but I reluctantly told this man what I believed God was leading me to do. During that year of obedience, I suffered. Greatly. But in the midst of my pain, I learned some things about the man's character which had been hidden. The more I learned, the more I realized that God's answer to marrying him was a resounding no.

My heart was crushed, but it survived. Time passed and I healed. Then one day the sun came out and I met the one God said yes to and the one I could also say yes to! This time the fruit of the relationship was only love, joy, and peace. God's blessing was so evident on our relationship that the entire family blessed it. Before his father, a retired pastor, had even met me he told my husband, "My only question is: Why haven't you married her yet?" What a joyful day it was when he, along with my new brother-in-law, laid hands of blessing on our hands and joined us in holy matrimony.

Even as I tell this story, I get emotional. I am so thankful to God for helping me learn obedience through suffering. Though I pounded my fists against walls and cried out to Him for my will, I am forever grateful that I chose His instead.

To become all God created us to be, there are some things only He can do for us and there are other things that only we can do. The Lord will empower us by His Spirit to walk in righteousness, but ultimately to have a changed life, we must obey God.

"If you love Me, keep My commandments." (John 14:15)

Though we may not like the word *obedience* and the images it conjures up, the Lord knows it is key to living in the fullness of His joy! Like Jesus who "learned obedience by the things which He suffered" (Heb. 5:8), I suffered when I was following a path which was not God's best for me. However, now I praise God for that suffering. Though I didn't know it at the time, the Lord was protecting me from situations that would have damaged my life and the lives of others!

Obedience is the doorway through which we must walk to find God's very best. Only by trusting and obeying Him can we come into the amazing abundant life He has destined for us!

Father, I know what I want, but You know what I need. Give me the courage to obey you today even if it hurts! Help me love You more and trust that your purposes for me are good. Thank you for helping me fulfill my high calling in Christ, for it is in His holy name that I pray, amen.

1. What is the difference between punishment and discipline?

2. Was there a time in your life when you didn't obey God? What happened?

3. What is the Lord asking you to do today to obey Him?

DAY THIRTY

Growing in Godliness

Have you ever wished you could have a conversation with a younger version of yourself? Now a grandmother, I can look back and see the things I would change about myself in earlier years. How much struggle I would have spared myself and others if I had learned obedience to the Lord in the small, seemingly insignificant details of life!

It's easy to say we believe on Sunday mornings, but our faith is really measured in how we live the rest of the week. True worship honors God in both the spiritual and the mundane things of life. Are we able to be good stewards of His gifts? Are we surrendering everything to Him, including our bodies, our minds, our relationships, our finances, and even our time management? The Lord wants to bring His order and peace into every area of our lives. He wants to get into our personal business!

> *Giving all diligence, add to your faith virtue, to virtue knowledge, to knowledge self-control, to self-control perseverance, to perseverance godliness, to godliness brotherly kindness, and to brotherly kindness love. For if these things are yours and abound, you will be neither barren nor unfruitful in the knowledge of our Lord Jesus Christ. (2 Peter 1:5–8)*

Growing in godliness would be easy if the Lord did all the work, but Peter reminds us that becoming all God made us to be requires personal responsibility. We are accountable for our attitudes and actions not only in church but also at home and at work. We honor the Lord when we are prudent with our spending, when we manage our home and family well, and even as we care for our bodies! True faith involves willingness to grow in wisdom, diligence, self-control, and perseverance.

Without a desire to grow in godliness we miss out on so many blessings God designed us to enjoy. For example, people often ask me to pray for physical healing without acknowledging how personal choices have affected their health. Some have abused their bodies with poor eating habits or addictions and then can't understand why they aren't healed. The miraculous answer they seek is not in a magic prayer, but rather in learning to be a good steward of the Lord's temple.

Others seek financial miracles but are deeply in debt due to foolish spending. They pray for deliverance from their difficulty yet aren't willing to take responsibility for the choices that got them there in the first place. Financial blessing comes as we honor God with what He provides.

Some ask the Lord to bless their public ministry while concealing a personal sin, perhaps an addiction to pornography and lust. Our God is not impressed with good works—He is looking for virtue! True holiness is letting the Lord be glorified in our lives even when no one is looking.

Religion is an outward appearance of worship but not necessarily the real thing. The Lord isn't interested in religion—He's looking for those who will worship Him *in spirit and in truth* (see John 4:24). We show God we *really* love Him by obeying His Word. He asks for surrendered hearts, not to make us slaves but so we might receive our full inheritance as sons and daughters! Whenever we say no to the Lord, we miss out on a piece of the abundant life He has prepared for us.

> *"And you shall love the LORD your God with all your heart, with all your soul, with all your mind, and with all your strength." This is the first commandment. (Mark 12:30)*

Even as I write these words, the Holy Spirit is convicting me of ways I could be more faithful. Salvation is a one-time experience, but sanctification, or being made holy, is a lifelong process. Until we get to heaven, the Holy Spirit will always be revealing those places in our hearts that are not yet fully submitted to Him. Our job is to humbly accept correction and allow the Lord to rule and reign in us, both in public and in private. Let's ask the Lord to show us where we need more of Him and the courage to change!

Father, I know there are areas of my life I have not fully surrendered to You. I desire to love You with all of my heart, soul, mind, and strength! Help me accept the leading of the Holy Spirit to become all You have made me to be. In Jesus' name, amen.

1. For some, this may be the hardest chapter of the book to read and accept. Why is it easier for us to do religious things than to admit that we need help with areas such as taking care of our house, bodies, or finances?

2. Why is it easier to judge others than to truthfully evaluate ourselves?

3. What are some areas of your life where you need to grow in discipline, self-control, and holiness?

DAY THIRTY-ONE

Sowing for a Harvest

When I made my first CD, I was a single mother living in poverty. Still, I prayed and the Lord provided the needed money to not only pay the bills but also record music. After the CD was finished, I felt that God was leading me to give away the proceeds from the sales as an offering to Him. Oh, how I did not want to hear those words! I assumed I needed this income for my family, but the Lord provided and eventually it gave me great joy to share the blessings I had received. It was such a privilege that year to give offerings to local and international missions and to know that my little gift could make a difference in lives of people I may never meet.

For the next recording project, I was bolder in my faith and asked the Lord for a full orchestra, an Irish producer, and great musicians to join me. The price tag for this was more than I could earn in a year, but again the Lord faithfully provided all I asked for! Since that time, the Lord has graciously opened the doors to record many more CDs with incredible musicians from around the world.

I have often wondered if the blessing of His provision was related to that very first offering. Would God have continued to give the increase without my faithfulness to His leading? I may never know, but deep in my heart I believe God provided as I obeyed in my giving back to Him.

Our human nature is to tightly hold on to what we possess when we believe there may not be enough. In the Bible, however, the Lord always brought blessing and increase upon that which was given away! The Scriptures show God providing for a lowly widow as she gave her last meal to the prophet Elijah (see 1 Kings 17). Jesus praised another widow who put the entirety of her life savings into the temple treasury (see Luke 21). When a young boy freely gave up his lunch, Jesus blessed it and then transformed it into enough food to feed thousands (see John 6:1–14).

What I love about this miracle is that it happened not in Jesus' hands, but rather in the hands of those who distributed the bread. Surely the twelve men were also hungry, but instead of eating, they were told to give away the little that they held in their hands!

What a test of faith, but in the end their faith was rewarded as there were twelve baskets of food leftover, one for each disciple. In the same way, God can take our little morsels and turn them into brimming baskets of food as we give with generous hearts. What a great deal!

> *"Give, and it will be given to you: good measure, pressed down, shaken together, and running over will be put into your bosom. For with the same measure that you use, it will be measured back to you." (Luke 6:38)*

We are sowing seeds for a harvest when we give Him our best in every area of our lives. As we share mercy we receive mercy. As we give of our finances, the Lord provides. As we sow kindness, kindness is in turn given back to us. As we bless others, we posture ourselves to receive blessing, wholeness, increase, and transformation!

Are there areas of your life where you feel stuck and unable to move forward? Do you need change in your marriage, your finances, your job, or just life in general? I challenge you to think of ways to give out of your poverty. That's right, give not out of your abundance, but from the area where you are lacking!

When we give, we are loving God and trusting Him to take care of our every need. Our gifts of money, time, words, and actions become seeds that we sow in faith. As we offer everything we have to the Lord, we position ourselves to receive all He has for us!

> *He who sows sparingly will also reap sparingly, and he who sows bountifully will also reap bountifully. So let each one give as he purposes in his heart, not grudgingly or of necessity; for God loves a cheerful giver. And God is able to make all grace abound toward you, that you, always having all sufficiency in all things, may have an abundance for every good work. (2 Cor. 9:6–8)*

Father, forgive me for holding onto what I have instead of giving as You lead. Help me to love as You love and to give as You give. Help me to trust Your love and realize that I can never outgive You. Lord, make me into an outrageous giver! In Your name I pray, amen.

1. Why is the heart of the giver more important than the gift itself?

2. How does giving change our hearts?

3. What should our attitude be as we give? Is it right to give in order to receive?

DAY THIRTY-TWO

Lifestyle of Worship

Winters are hard here in Michigan, and I am often grounded from travel in January and February. Though I don't always enjoy having my wings clipped, staying home for a few weeks is probably a good thing! I am the type of person who likes to be on the go, but at times I have sensed the Lord telling me to slow down and just be. He has inspired me to worship Him, not just in exciting mountaintop experiences but also in the simple, ordinary moments of everyday life.

I am reminded of a story in the Bible when Jesus was traveling in the middle of the day. The disciples had gone to buy lunch and Jesus was thirsty, so He went to a well for a drink. The Lord sat down at the well and soon a Samaritan woman came to draw water. He asked the woman for a drink, and she gave it to Him. In that very moment, the simple act of sharing water became an offering to the living God!

"Woman, believe Me, the hour is coming when you will neither on this mountain, nor in Jerusalem, worship the Father. . . . But the hour is coming, and now is, when the true worshipers will worship the Father in spirit and truth; for the Father is seeking such to worship Him. God is Spirit, and those who worship Him must worship in spirit and truth."

The woman said to Him, "I know that Messiah is coming" (who is called Christ). "When He comes, He will tell us all things."

Jesus said to her, "I who speak to you am He." (John 4:21, 23–26)

The Samaritan woman never imagined she would meet her Savior on an ordinary day in the midst her chores. As she unknowingly served God, her eyes were opened and she saw Him for who He really was!

I am learning that this is a picture of true worship. It's easy to praise God during an inspiring worship service with great music and anointed preaching. But God is looking for those who will worship Him not just on Sunday morning, but even on a Monday morning while dwelling in the valley.

If we look carefully, we can see the Lord's holiness even in the ordinary things of life—His beauty in a sunrise, His joy in the laughter of a child, and His strength in our daily chores.

When our hearts are focused on the Lord, suddenly even the dust under our feet becomes holy ground!

Earth's crammed with heaven,
And every bush afire with God
But only he who sees, takes off his shoes,
The rest sit round it, and pluck blackberries.

—Elizabeth Browning

The Lord is constantly revealing Himself to us. We are the ones who miss His presence because we are so focused on ourselves and on the worries and cares of life. We expect to find God only in the spectacular, and yet we forget that He *is* spectacular, and He is all around us. In fact, He seems to prefer working miracles in ordinary places where ordinary folks live, work, and love. Take a moment and close your eyes. Can you sense His presence? Just know that wherever you are, He is there with you.

Learning to live in the awareness of God's presence takes time and practice. The more we train our hearts to worship the Lord as we go about our day, the more He will fill us with the living water of the Holy Spirit.

". . . whoever drinks of the water that I shall give him will never thirst. But the water that I shall give him will

become in him a fountain of water springing up into everlasting life." (John 4:14)

As we make a conscious decision to seek Christ in each moment, our hearts can be filled with heaven while our feet are still on earth. I want to be so full of the Holy Spirit that one day I will close my eyes in this world and open them in the next finding only the scenery has changed! We may not always like the scenery here on earth, but if we look with the eyes of our hearts, we can behold His beauty in every moment and every place.

Lord, thank You for interrupting my busyness and reminding me of what is truly important. Help me stay focused on eternal things and teach me how to worship You in my thoughts, words, and actions. Be a fountain of living water in me today! In Jesus' name I pray, amen.

1. How does worship change the worshiper?

2. How could worship affect the lives of those around us?

3. What does it mean to worship God in spirit and truth?

DAY THIRTY-THREE

The Greatest of These

God will change our hearts as we surrender to Him. He will change our situations as we pray, but He changes our relationships as we love. Love is our boots-on-the-ground weapon against Satan! It breaks his power, one stronghold at a time, and totally disarms him!

So what does it really mean to love someone? Hollywood portrays love as a self-gratifying feeling that comes and goes. But Jesus came into the world to show us a higher level of love. He taught us that if we truly love someone, we will lay down our life down for that person (see John 15:13).

Satan is crushed under our feet as we *wash the feet of the one who has hurt us.* The person who has offended us doesn't have to apologize or even deserve our love. The power of Christ in us enables us to love *first.*

But God demonstrates His own love toward us, in that while we were still sinners, Christ died for us. (Rom. 5:8)

I have seen God heal many relationships when one person took the initiative to love the one who had mistreated them. This doesn't mean allowing someone to abuse us over and over again, but it does mean loving that person the way Jesus would.

In my own life, I have learned this lesson the hard way. Tired of living under my rules, my oldest daughter, Grace, left home when she was only eighteen years old. I knew she had met a young man, so I was not entirely surprised when just a few months later she broke the news to me that she was pregnant.

I was disappointed, crushed, embarrassed, and angry at both her and her boyfriend, Alex. Especially Alex. For several days I remember thinking that I never cared to see him again! That week in my devotional time, the Holy Spirit led me to read the entire book of First John, and so I did. The next day I tried to pray but sensed He was telling me to read it again, so I read it again. This continued and by the fourth day, I was getting *really tired* of reading First John. However, I kept noticing certain words jumping off the page: "If someone says, 'I love God,' and hates his brother, he is a liar; for he who does not love his brother whom he has seen, how can he love God whom he has not seen?" (1 John 4:20).

"But I don't hate anyone!" I said defensively to the Lord. I could almost imagine Him saying, "Oh really, are you sure about that?" So, I prayed that the Lord would change my heart toward Grace and Alex. I never realized though, that changing my heart would involve action.

When I prayed about it, I continued to sense the Lord leading me to invite them out to eat. My first thought was, *Invite them out? I don't even want to spend my time or money on them! Maybe I'll just invite them over for chili.* But the Lord was very clear that I was to invite them out specifically to the nearby Cracker Barrel restaurant for Sunday lunch. So I reluctantly gave in and called Grace.

She and Alex were surprised, but agreed to have lunch with me that Sunday. When we first saw each other there was an awkward silence and I could tell they were uncomfortable. But I reached through the silence and hugged them both, telling them I was understandably disappointed but would love and support them and my new grandchild as we moved forward. Alex, surprised by my words, smiled with relief and said, "You know, Cracker Barrel is my favorite restaurant!" At that moment, I knew God was grinning!

I learned that the way I responded to this crisis would either show them the grace of God or push them away in judgment. How could I judge their sins when I have plenty of my own? Showing mercy opened the door for a beautiful family relationship as my husband later married them in our backyard!

We can allow hurts and offenses to destroy us or we can use them to destroy Satan's plans by responding in love. When we choose to sow mercy, we will reap a harvest of mercy in our own lives!

> *And now abide faith, hope, love, these three; but the greatest of these is love. (1 Cor. 13:13)*

Lord, give me the courage to love as You love. Help me follow Your example and lay down my life for those who have hurt me. O God, love them through me! In Jesus' name, amen.

1. How is true love a force and not just a feeling?

2. Write down or share a time when you did not deserve love, but God loved you anyway.

3. Is there someone in your life right now that needs to know the love of Christ through you?

PART FOUR

Calling Forth Change

DAY THIRTY-FOUR

Calling Forth Change

Change happens within us as God's Word takes root in our hearts. Change happens in others as His Word touches them through us. Finally, change happens in the world as we call forth the Lord's Word through prayer!

> *"Lord, teach us to pray, as John also taught his disciples."*
>
> *So He said to them, "When you pray, say: Our Father in heaven, hallowed be Your name. Your kingdom come. Your will be done on earth as it is in heaven. Give us day by day our daily bread. And forgive us our sins, for we also forgive everyone who is indebted to us. And do not lead us into temptation, but deliver us from the evil one." (Luke 11:1–4)*

There have been times when I wondered why prayer was necessary. Why does God tell us to ask for things as if He is a divine vending machine ready to take our orders? Many times my prayers have gone unanswered, so what's the point? I may not completely understand why God asks us to pray, but I know from experience that He hears our prayers!

Having suffered due to a cross-country move and family trauma, my oldest son, Charlie, began experimenting with drugs when he was only twelve years old. One day he came home on the school bus with marijuana and before long he was addicted to cocaine, crystal meth, cigarettes, alcohol, and anything else that could numb his pain. My heart broke as I saw him turn to the wrong crowd and self-harm for comfort.

So I did what every self-respecting but desperate Christian mom does: I prayed. At first my prayers were loud and confident, but as the months turned into years, nothing changed in Charlie's life, and I grew weary. Even the police, who knew us all too well, told me that Charlie stood little chance of getting free of drugs and would either die or land in prison. Finally, after five years of prayer, I had all but lost hope.

Falling on my knees, I cried out, "God, I know it's not Your will for my son to die of drug addiction. Please show me Your strategy to win this war!" The Lord answered my prayer by reminding me of a story in the Bible. It was the account of Moses instructing the Israelites to paint the blood of a lamb on their doorposts and lintels. As the blood was applied, all in the household were saved from death (see Exodus 12:13). At that moment I knew God was telling me that I had spiritual authority over my household. Although I didn't understand much about spiritual warfare, I believed that I had authority to fight for my son's life through prayer!

The next few days were spent listening for the Lord's marching orders. While praying, I kept hearing the number five in my mind and so I told a few friends I would fast for five days. Four of them joined me and we spiritually painted the blood of the Lamb on the doorposts and lintels of the house! We believed Satan had no right to my children, and so we fervently prayed that the stronghold of addiction in Charlie's life would be broken.

As we prayed and fasted, the atmosphere in the house was intense, like fingernails on a chalkboard. Charlie came to me, pleading for us to stop. He was hearing voices saying they would kill him if we continued. If I didn't believe in the demonic realm before, I certainly did now! I told Charlie the voices were lying to him and that we would not stop.

By the fifth day, we were all hungry and exhausted and Charlie was still addicted. That night, he went to bed high on cocaine and I went to bed feeling low and hopeless. But the next morning he woke me saying, "Mom, get up, something happened. Jesus appeared in my room last night!"

My son who had gone to bed intoxicated was now completely sober. He proclaimed, "I threw my cigarettes and drugs away. He set me free!" I wasn't sure I believed him at first, but the next thing I knew he was at the shopping mall giving Bibles away. He was looking for drug addicts to tell them what Jesus had done for him!

So after five years of praying and five people fasting for five days, my son was set free in 2005 from the bondage of drug addiction. I later learned that the number five represents grace in the Bible, and grace is what we received! The Lord showed me how to fight the battle not in my own strength, but in His.

I tell this story to encourage you to keep praying until you see God's kingdom established in your life, your marriage, your home, your community, and your world. Often we don't pray because we don't really believe our prayers are effective. True, our prayers accomplish nothing if they are just words, but when we pray in agreement with God's will by the power of the Holy Spirit, miracles can happen!

> *The effective, fervent prayer of a righteous man avails much. (James 5:16b)*

I hope you are encouraged to believe that with God all things truly are possible. His kingdom will come in our lives and the lives of our loved ones as we call it forth in prayer!

Lord, teach me how to pray so I may lay hold of Your perfect will for my life and for my world. Give me the strength and perseverance to pray and keep praying until Your Word is established on earth! In Jesus' name, amen.

1. How does prayer change the one who prays as much or even more than the one who is prayed for?

2. Matthew 18:19 says, "If two of you on earth agree about anything they ask for, it will be done for them by my Father in heaven" (NIV). Why is it so important to have people to pray with?

3. It can often be a struggle to make time to pray. How can we become more disciplined in our prayer life?

DAY THIRTY-FIVE

Shameless Audacity

I am convinced that without prayer my son would have never been delivered from drug addiction and may have even died. The answered prayer did not come because my friends and I had great faith, but simply because we didn't give up! We all have parts of our lives that don't quite look like heaven yet because we often settle for too little. We have not because we ask not (see James 4:2) or because we quit too soon!

> *Ask and keep on asking and it will be given to you; seek and keep on seeking and you will find; knock and keep on knocking and the door will be opened to you. (Matt. 7:7 AMP)*

Because of Jesus' sacrifice on the cross, those who believe are sons and daughters of the Father and coheirs with Christ. Through Him by prayer, we have access to the throne room of heaven. To put it simply, when we pray, God listens! Not because He must but because He promised. So we have the capacity to touch the heart of God and call forth His kingdom on the earth. Just as Queen Esther had access to the throne room and moved the heart of the king, perhaps we have been brought to royal position for such a time as this (see Esther 4:14)! Can you imagine what would happen if we all prayed for God's kingdom to come in our own little spheres of influence? The course of history would be changed through our prayers!

Jesus not only encouraged His disciples to pray with persistence but also with boldness. In Luke 11:5–8, He said, "Suppose you have a friend, and you go to him at midnight and say, 'Friend, lend me three loaves of bread; a friend of mine on a journey has come to me, and I have no food to offer him.' And suppose the one inside answers, 'Don't bother me. The door is already locked, and my children and I are in bed. I can't get up and give you anything.' I tell you, even though he will not get up and give you the bread because of friendship, yet because of your shameless audacity he will surely get up and give you as much as you need" (NIV).

It doesn't offend God when we continually ask for something in prayer. In fact, I'm sure we frustrate Him when we *don't* ask, for this shows our unbelief. Jesus commended the shameless audacity of the friend in the parable, and He is looking for those with this same boldness to keep praying until His love is fully revealed on the earth! Our prayers truly can move the heart of God.

In another account, Jesus was so touched by a woman's request that He changed His mind! A Canaanite woman came and begged Jesus to deliver her daughter from demons. Knowing He was not yet called to preach the kingdom of God to the Gentiles, "He answered and said, 'It is not good to take the children's bread and throw it to the little dogs.' And she said, 'Yes, Lord, yet even the little dogs eat the crumbs which fall from their masters' table.' Then Jesus answered and said to her, 'O woman, great is your faith! Let it be to you as you desire.' And her daughter was healed from that very hour" (Matt. 15:26–28). The Canaanite woman trusted Jesus' heart so much that she asked Him to break the rules for her sake. Jesus was delighted by her faith and granted her request!

I wonder how much I have missed in the past because I was lazy, apathetic, or simply lacked the faith to pray and keep on praying. Remember that prayer is more about the process than the answer. The process of praying builds faith in the one who prays. It draws us closer to God and causes us to desire Him even more than we desire the answer to our request. We don't always get what we ask for, but God always rewards the one who continually seeks Him.

In the book of Genesis, Jacob wrestled with God saying, "I will not let you go until you bless me" (32:26 NIV). Is there an area in your life where you are struggling? Are you wrestling with God for the answer? Don't give up until you see His very best!

Father, forgive me for not always trusting Your love and believing for Your answers to my prayers. Forgive me for giving up too soon! Give me the courage to ask and ask and keep asking. In Jesus' name, amen.

1. In Matthew 15, Jesus commended the Canaanite woman for her faith. What does this story teach us about the dynamics of prayer?

2. Why does God invite us to pray? Couldn't He just do His will on earth without us?

3. What about the times when our prayers aren't answered in the way we hope? Is it because we didn't pray with diligence?

DAY THIRTY-SIX

Praying for Our Desires

Sometimes we don't pray because we can't believe our prayers will really make a difference. Other times we fail to pray because we've become too complacent or we're afraid of being disappointed. When we do pray, it's often easier to default to a safe and generic, "Thy will be done," instead of asking for what we really long for. Perhaps we have forgotten we serve a heavenly Father who loves and desires to bless us, His children! In fact, it is He who created us to have desires in the first place.

My earliest desires in life had everything to do with horses. Growing up I don't remember a time when I didn't love horses . . . and I don't even know why I loved them! I asked Santa for a pony when I was three (and didn't get one, much to my disappointment). My plan was to put him in a refrigerator box on the porch! The obsession continued until my parents finally relented and let me take riding lessons when I was nine years old. Not able to have a horse of my own, I would clean stalls at the stable and do whatever I could just to ride a horse that wasn't being used. I was happy to ride anything with four legs and often rode the mounts no one else wanted.

As an adult, horses were no longer part of my life but were always part of my dreams. I began volunteering at a local Christian equestrian center just for the chance to be around them again. My daughters also caught the equestrian bug and as young children they enjoyed collecting plastic horses. However, as they grew older, they lost interest in toys and allowed me to give some of them away. One day as I was packing away these neglected toys, one little horse caught my attention. He was a small black horse with one white foot and a white mark on his nose. This little plastic toy made me smile so I placed it on the dresser in my room.

The girls made fun of me, saying, "Mom, why do you have a toy horse?"

"I don't know—I just like that one. Now leave me alone!" I said, laughing at myself along with them. Looking at the plastic horse stirred something within my heart to pray that one day God would give me a real horse of my own. This was my dream, but as a single mom it seemed like an impossible request!

Then one day a new horse showed up at the stable where I volunteered. She was a yearling who had been rescued from the meat buyers at a horse auction. Although she was wild looking and untrained, to me this delicate filly was strikingly beautiful! Rosie, as she was called, was a black bay with one white foot and a white mark on her nose. I couldn't help noticing how much she reminded me of the toy on my dresser. She was then taken to another stable for training but a year later she came back, still fearful and extremely difficult to handle.

At that time, I was going through a painful period in life because of a broken relationship and I was also fearful and difficult to handle. One day I went out into the pasture just to be alone and cry. As I sat with my back against a saddle, I heard a horse breathing behind me. It was Rosie! She came alongside me and laid her head against my cheek, staying several minutes as if to comfort me in my pain.

Not long after that, the stable manager suggested I work with Rosie to see if I could get her accustomed to being handled. So knowing that Rosie's love language was touch, I began hands-on training every day, teaching her to trust me. Soon I was leading her through challenging obstacles, and she was gaining confidence. Within six weeks she had a saddle on her back, and I was riding her!

Rosie's owner saw the bond between us and offered her to me as a gift. "She's your horse!" she declared, amazed at the progress Rosie had made. Another friend offered to help pay for her feed, and Rosie officially became mine. We learned later that this beautiful animal had championship bloodlines but unfortunately had ended up in the wrong place at the wrong time—or perhaps it was the right place in God's right time!

The Lord had created Rosie for a purpose and created me with a desire. The little plastic horse I kept on my dresser was a model of the gift God was preparing for me! As we delight ourselves in the Lord, He delights to give us the desires of our hearts.

I continue to learn many new things with Rosie. There is so much trust between us that at times I have been able to ride her with no bridle—controlling her only with my voice and legs. She loves to please me, and I love to lavish my affection on her. It also doesn't hurt her feelings to have a carrot or an apple to reward her good behavior!

Rosie is a beautiful reminder of how God lavishes His love on us every day if we simply allow Him! He takes great pleasure in fulfilling the desires of our hearts. We may not always get what we want when we pray, but we can trust that He will give us His very best. In Christ, He can surely fulfill our wants, our needs, and His perfect will.

> *Every good gift and every perfect gift is from above, and comes down from the Father of lights, with whom there is no variation or shadow of turning. (James 1:17)*

Father, You know the desires of my heart and that ultimately my heart is only fulfilled in You! Teach me to love You more and to choose what You desire. As I pray, I trust You to give me what is best. In Jesus' name, amen.

1. Why bother to pray for our desires rather than just praying for God's will to be done?

2. What do specific answers to prayer teach us about God's love?

3. Think of a time you prayed for something specific and how God answered your prayer. How did the answer—whether you received what you asked for or not—affect your understanding of God's love?

DAY THIRTY-SEVEN

Garment of Praise

The answers to our prayers don't always come right away. It's easy to grow weary or afraid while we wait for change! If allowed, the pain of waiting for what we hope for in the future can prevent us from enjoying the Lord's presence today. That is exactly what Satan wants! He knows that when we continue to worship God, regardless of the outcome of our prayers, spiritual strongholds will fall.

For years, I had a wounded relationship with a dear friend. There was a mutual misunderstanding and broken communication. I tried everything to bridge the gap, but all that remained was the painful loss of a precious friendship. Late one night I awoke from a deep sleep. I was in pain and began to cry out to the Lord for restoration of the damaged relationship. However the more I prayed, the more upset I became! I later realized that my prayers were flowing from fear rather than faith.

Doesn't she know she is wrong? I pondered. *When I wake up in the morning, I am going to text her and tell her,* in love, *that she needs to reconcile with God and with me.*

At that point, I was so worried and frustrated that I thought only of myself. Fortunately, in the midst of my turmoil, I was able to hear the Holy Spirit speak to my heart: "What if you took all this time and energy you just wasted fretting and worshiped Me?"

Taken aback, I suddenly realized that because my heart was full of fear, trusting God was the furthest thing from my mind. So I found my iPod in the dark and turned on worship music. Before long, I had forgotten my distress and was immersed in the presence of God! Enveloped in His love and peace, I finally fell asleep.

When I awoke in the morning, my headphones were laying on the pillow and I had forgotten what upset me . . . but the Lord hadn't forgotten. I reached for the phone and, to my amazement, a text message was waiting there for me from the very person I was about to rebuke!

"Hey Jean, you have been on my heart a lot lately. Just wanted you to know that I love you, and I am praying for you. Let's get together soon."

While worshiping in the middle of the night, the Lord had shifted something in her heart . . . and more importantly in my heart! I shudder to think what further damage I would have caused had I taken matters into my own hands. Spiritual battles are never won with human strength. Worry and fear only empower the enemy! Strongholds fall by faith, and faith expressed through worship is our greatest weapon against evil.

In Second Chronicles 20, the army of Judah was surrounded by its enemies and facing certain defeat. King Jehoshaphat, however, believed that the Lord would fight and win the battle for them. In faith, he commanded the singers to be sent in front of the army *with only the weapon of praise*. As they marched forward praising God with loud voices, their enemies fled in confusion and eventually destroyed each other! This is one of many accounts in the Bible where the Lord saved His people as they chose to praise Him *first*. Walls fell, giants were slain, and armies were routed as men and women demonstrated that the Lord was their strength through their praise. When they put their trust in God, He won the victory for them!

Every day we face new battles and so often we try to fight them ourselves instead of letting God defend us. When faced with a difficult situation, we will find our strength on our knees with hands raised to heaven in worship. Praise confuses the enemy and sends him running because Satan can't stick around when the Lord is near!

Regardless of where you need transformation in your life, I encourage you to stop fretting *about* the situation and start praising God *in* that situation. If you feel overwhelmed by darkness, then turn on His light by worshiping Him! Don't wait for the victory to be won because the Lord is worthy of our praise regardless of the outcome. As you place Him above your personal desires, He will bring about His desires for you.

> *But thanks be to God, who gives us the victory through our Lord Jesus Christ. (1 Cor. 15:57)*

Father, forgive me for fearing others more than I trust You. Forgive me for focusing on myself rather than worshiping You. In this moment I choose to exalt You above my battles and above my own desires. I trust You to bring your kingdom in Your way and Your time! In Jesus' name, amen.

1. How could worshiping God be considered spiritual warfare?

2. Why would the spiritual forces of darkness be afraid of a worshiping Christian?

3. What is the difference between praying for something in faith and praying for something in fear?

DAY THIRTY-EIGHT

Fasting for Breakthrough

As I prayed for my son to be delivered from his drug addiction, I was keenly aware of the intense spiritual battle going on. Charlie was in bondage to his flesh and to spiritual forces of darkness that had gained power in his life. No amount of effort on his part would have set him free. Freedom from spiritual bondage requires spiritual warfare through prayer.

> *For we do not wrestle against flesh and blood, but against principalities, against powers, against the rulers of the darkness of this age, against spiritual hosts of wickedness in the heavenly places. (Eph. 6:12)*

However, sometimes prayer alone is not enough to break the spiritual strongholds. Once, Jesus' disciples prayed, but they were not able to cast a demon out of a young boy. When they asked Jesus why their prayers were ineffective, He said, "This kind can come out by nothing but prayer and fasting" (Mark 9:29).

Few churches talk about fasting anymore. Our me-centered, self-gratifying culture doesn't want to hear about depriving the flesh! And yet fasting was a regular part of the lives of our spiritual forefathers. Jesus prepared for His own public ministry by fasting for forty days and nights. He also taught about fasting as a regular part of the life of a Jewish believer.

> *"When you fast, do not look somber as the hypocrites do, for they disfigure their faces to show others they are fasting. Truly I tell you, they have received their reward in full. But when you fast, put oil on your head and wash your face, so that it will not be obvious to others that you are fasting, but only to your Father, who is unseen; and your Father, who sees what is done in secret, will reward you." (Matt. 6:16–18 NIV)*

Fasting was not something that Jesus commanded us to do, but He did say that fasting with a right spirit would bring reward. It causes us to draw closer to Him and helps us to hear His voice more clearly. There is no set formula telling us how long to fast, and there are many different ways to fast. The important thing is to follow the Holy Spirit's leading.

In my own life, times of fasting have brought tremendous growth and breakthrough. Did fasting cause my son to be delivered from drugs? No, I don't believe we have that kind of power. Prayer and fasting simply enlarges our faith to be able to receive God's highest will. *The key to answered prayer through fasting is not asking for something from God, but rather simply asking for more of Him.*

Fasting changes our focus from the earthly to the heavenly. As we fix our hearts on God, our faith begins to grow. When we feel physically hungry, we can declare to the Lord that we love Him more than the food our bodies crave. As we subdue the flesh, our spiritual sight becomes more focused and so do our prayers. When we pray in agreement with God's Spirit, the mountains in our lives will surely move!

Do you have a mountain that needs to move? Do you need direction in your life or strength for a trying situation? Perhaps you have a loved one who needs the Lord or a friend who is struggling with a life-threatening disease. If you are overwhelmed with an earthly need, I encourage you to reach higher and ask for more of God. He will bless you with His presence, His comfort, His power, and His guidance.

As you fast you will begin to clearly hear from God and breakthroughs will take place. You will experience God's love more intensely as your physical hunger is replaced with spiritual hunger. Jesus said that those who hunger and thirst for righteousness are blessed and they will be filled!

Father, I come to You with many needs and desires. My struggles are sometimes more than I can bear. Please give me the grace to fast and pray for Your answers, not mine. I trust You to give me Your very best as I seek You first. In Jesus' name, amen.

1. How could fasting intensify our prayers?

2. Is it possible to fast with wrong motives?

3. What other types of fasting (besides abstaining from eating) might be beneficial in our spiritual life from time to time?

DAY THIRTY-NINE

In the Waiting

Although prayer and fasting were vital in my son's deliverance, the spiritual warfare for Charlie began when he was just a small boy. Charlie's full name means "strong little warrior," and from the moment he was born little Charles Wyatt lived up to his name. By the time he was only two years old, this strong-willed child had brought me to my knees in frustration! Fortunately, as I prayed with a friend late one night, the Lord spoke His word to us about Charlie. Actually, the word came as a song by Rosemary Hilvers called "The Zeal of God":

The zeal of God will consume him, it will burn within his soul
A driving force that cannot be stopped, a fire that cannot be quenched . . .

Throughout his childhood, I sang those words to Charlie every night before he went to sleep. Hundreds of times, my son heard who God said he was and who he was to become one day in Christ. Little did I know that this simple song would eventually save Charlie's life!

Years later when he was a teenager bound up in addiction, everyone told Charlie that he was a failure and a lost cause. I recall picking him up once after he had been caught shoplifting. I brought him home and then saw him weeping as he looked at himself in the mirror. It was as if the blinders were off, and he could finally see who he had become without God.

I remember putting my arms around him and softly singing into his ear, "The zeal of God will consume you . . ." and he said, "Mom, I want to be free!" Now completely broken, Charlie was ready to become the man God had made him to be! My friends and I began fasting and praying, and in one miraculous encounter his heart and life were changed forever.

Sometimes the Lord brings change instantaneously and other times it is a process. In some cases no matter how much we pray, nothing seems to happen. We plead with God for miracles and hear only silence! As physical beings, we forget that the Lord is at work even when we don't see anything happening.

When he was seventy-five years old, God promised Abraham he would be the father of many nations, but he would have to wait another twenty-five years for the promise to be fulfilled. During this time, the Lord was shaping Abraham into a man of faith, strength, and endurance who would truly be worthy to be called the father of many nations. God's timing is always perfect!

Moses was forty years old when he fled Egypt, but it was another forty years before the Lord called him to return. During those years in the wilderness, Moses' heart was softened to hear the voice of God and then prepared to obey it. God's timing is always perfect!

Even Jesus was born to save us from our sins in the fullness of time (see Galatians 4:4). There were four hundred years of silence between the final words of the prophets and Christ's birth. Only the Father knew the right moment for His salvation to appear in our sinful world and also in our lives. God's timing is always perfect!

We pray for the immediate fulfillment of our desires, but just because we don't see the answer right away doesn't mean God is not at work. Just as a seed sends roots into the darkness of the soil before the plant appears, the Lord is also working in our darkness so He can bring forth His fruit into the light! So, let us not grow weary as we wait for God. As we wait, He is preparing our hearts to receive His very best.

But those who wait on the Lord shall renew their strength; they shall mount up with wings like eagles, they shall run and not be weary, they shall walk and not faint. (Isa. 40:31)

Father, You know what I hope and wait for. Thank You for hearing and listening to my prayers! Prepare and strengthen my heart to receive Your answer in Your perfect time. In Jesus' name, amen.

1. What is God's view of time?

2. Why is time an important element in developing our faith for answered prayer?

3. Think of an answer to prayer that you had to wait for. How would things have turned out differently if you had not had to wait?

DAY FORTY

Made in His Image

Well, we've made it to end of our forty-day divine experiment! Has your life changed the way you hoped it would? Are you excited to continue on this road, or are you still a bit discouraged?

In the past when I became disheartened it was usually because my dreams and goals were not the Lord's dreams and goals for my life. With powerful words, the prophet Isaiah reminds us why Jesus came:

The Spirit of the Lord God is upon Me,
Because the Lord has anointed Me
To preach good tidings to the poor;
He has sent Me to heal the brokenhearted,
To proclaim liberty to the captives,
And the opening of the prison to those who are bound;

To proclaim the acceptable year of the LORD,
And the day of vengeance of our God;
To comfort all who mourn,
To console those who mourn in Zion,
To give them beauty for ashes,
The oil of joy for mourning,
The garment of praise for the spirit of heaviness;
That they may be called trees of righteousness,
The planting of the LORD, that He may be glorified.
(Isa. 61:1–3)

God's plan has never been to make us comfortable, happy, or perfect, although one day we will be all of these things. His highest calling is for us to *look like Jesus* so we can then show Him to the world. We desire complete transformation while on earth, but even when God doesn't answer our prayers the way we hope, His love is always at work deep within our hearts.

How tenderly He molds us and how carefully He shapes us! Only the Potter can see the beauty He is crafting in His humble lumps of clay. Patiently, He turns the wheel while applying just the right amount of pressure for the pot to rise within His hands. With the knife He carves, with His own blood He paints, and with the furnace He fires His porcelain masterpiece to completion. When He is satisfied, He holds it to the light. If fired correctly, He will see not the clay, but rather the Light shining through it. When He taps it, it rings . . . vibrating in perfect rhythm with the heart of the Potter!

My son Andrew is a potter, and he recently told me that fine porcelain clay produces the highest quality pottery. Yet to be both beautiful and usable it must be fired at extremely high temperatures. In like manner, the Lord desires to fashion us into beautiful and useful vessels for His service. In God's hands, pain can be a powerful tool transforming us into the image of Christ. Oh that we would admire His workmanship in us rather than resist the process!

I recently discovered the powerful story of Katherine Wolf, who suffered a major stroke at the age of twenty-six and then learned to overcome in the midst of crushing tragedy. She encourages those of us who hurt, "To *suffer well* allowing pain to be our tutor by teaching us what really matters in life." Katherine challenges us to see pain through the lens of God's love saying, "Don't waste your pain—cherish it! What if we take our brokenness and celebrate it? Suffering doesn't have to be the end of our story. Suffering is the beginning of a better story!"[1]

Last year I was dealing with a hurtful situation in my own life and simply wanted the stinging pain to stop. During this time the Holy Spirit spoke these words to my heart: "Why

---

1. Paraphrased from a speech located at https://youtu.be/x5OfPO3qo74?t=11m55s; words used begin at 12:02 and end around 13:53. Used with permission.

would you want to remove the nails that are holding you to the cross? I am using the very things that hurt you to make you more like Me."

When we suffer then . . .

> *Let us run with endurance the race that is set before us, looking unto Jesus, the author and finisher of our faith, who for the joy that was set before Him endured the cross, despising the shame, and has sat down at the right hand of the throne of God. (Heb. 12:1b–2)*

Jesus overcame the powers of darkness not only through His life, but also through His suffering, death, and triumphant resurrection. In the same way, we experience victory when we lay our lives down for His highest glory. May He receive all honor and praise as His life is revealed in us and through us!

Be encouraged my friend, for the Lord is doing such a marvelous work in you. I see it clearly right here from my kitchen table! In fact, when I look at you, *I see Jesus.*

> *But He knows the way that I take;*
> *When He has tested me, I shall come forth as gold. (Job 23:10)*

Father, thank You for sending Jesus to die for me that I might experience Your life, not just when I get to heaven but also here on earth. Help me receive the abundant life You have for me by giving me ears to hear, faith to believe, and courage to walk in obedience to Your Word. Most of all, thank You that You began this good work in me, and I know You will bring it to completion. In Jesus' name, amen.

1. James 1:2–4 says, "Consider it pure joy, my brothers and sisters, whenever you face trials of many kinds, because you know that the testing of your faith produces perseverance. Let perseverance finish its work so that you may be mature and complete, not lacking anything" (NIV). How is it possible to suffer and be joyful at the same time?

2. How does your response to suffering determine whether it destroys you or makes you stronger?

3. Think about a time in your life when you suffered. In what ways would you be different today if you had not endured that trial?

CPSIA information can be obtained
at www.ICGtesting.com
Printed in the USA
LVHW012158170521
687691LV00001B/1